Critical Mass
(The Dynamics of Discipleship)

By

Shane Sanders

© *2013*

PRESS

Critical Mass
(The Dynamics of Discipleship)
by Shane Sanders

Printed in the United States of America

ISBN 9781625094384

www.xulonpress.com

Critical Mass
(The Dynamics of Discipleship)

Preface

*R*edemption, growth, progress, change, transformation, multiplication, success—these are the fruits of critical mass in the context of Christian discipleship. This book presents a vision for discipleship, a philosophy of ministry, and a discussion of disciplemaking concepts and leadership priorities. I hope to take a fresh look at timeless truths and principles because the main thing is to *keep* the main thing the main thing. I also hope to be an encouragement, but I'm not referring to sympathy. To *encourage* is to put courage into, to motivate and fill with courage or strength of purpose, especially in preparation for an important mission. God encouraged Joshua to cross over the river and take the Promised Land, three times telling him to be strong and courageous (Joshua 1:1-9). With his command, he imparted strength and courage; he promised his continued presence; and he promised that Joshua's mission would be successful.

I'm reminded of a little-known biblical character named Archippus. He's only mentioned in two verses, Philemon 2 and Colossians 4:17, and he's one of three people addressed in the book of Philemon, including Philemon and Apphia who were likely his parents. The church of Colosse met in Philemon's home, so the two letters were related. Paul addressed Archippus in Philemon 2 as "our fellow soldier." He was a leader in the church, possibly the successor to its founder, Epaphras (Col. 1:7, 4:12, Phlem. 23). Paul's letter to the Colossians focused on the preeminence of Christ and the mystery of the ages–Christ in you, the hope of glory (Col. 1:27). But at the end of the letter, Paul singled out one person for a pointed challenge: "Say to Archippus, 'Take heed to the ministry which you have received in the Lord, that you may fulfill it'" (Col. 4:17, NASB). The success of Archippus' ministry hung in the balance, and was so crucial that it's forever recorded in Scripture.

Archippus was just an ordinary guy in a local ministry. What was so important about his mission? Take heed to the ministry you received in the Lord—fulfill your calling, complete your work! It was like Paul's challenge to Timothy to fulfill his ministry (2 Tim. 4:5). Paul called Archippus, a no-name ordinary guy, to faithful and persevering service in a mission of eternal importance. It was a challenge to go the distance, press to the goal, and run to win! Maybe the real issue for Archippus was that he needed encouragement and motivation to complete the race he started. Maybe he needed to be reminded how important his mission was—an ordinary guy from a local church on the *greatest* quest in history. And so do we!

I.

Key Concepts

1. Critical Mass

The chaos of the times is unprecedented. More people are alive today than have ever lived. The world population continues to grow, while global resources steadily shrink. Natural disasters have greatly increased. The world's economies are fragile, and the "have's" exploit the "have-nots." On top of all that, we're oppressed by the sophisticated technology that was supposed to make our lives easier. The mounting pressures and anxieties of modern life leave us gasping for air and racing to the brink. In this environment, understandably, people are engrossed in their needs and fears. Yet Christians are exhorted to seek first the kingdom of God and his righteousness, trusting that he will meet their needs (Matt. 6:33). But is that realistic in the modern age, and what truly is of *first* importance in life?

From Chaos to Critical Mass

Our natural tendency is to seek first our personal peace and affluence. It's hard to relate to a so-called eternal kingdom and the concept of holiness. These aren't terms we use in everyday language. They're religious terms. And we don't need another clichéd "plan for our lives." We do what we can and hope for best because the real world is harsh and complex, while the Christian life is extreme in its idealism. Maybe John Lennon was right—life is what happens to you when you're planning to do something else. *Or is it?* Can there be an over-arching plan for the ages, in place since the time before time, and orchestrated by a sovereign God? It's fun to imagine. It would at least give reason for hope or a diversion from reality. But is it true? *Oh yes, it is!*

As it turns out, we may be living in the most exciting times of all, near the climax of the ages when God *wins big!* So despite the current reign of chaos, the final victory is *not* in doubt. It won't even be close. The outcome does *not* hang in the balance. In fact, God has announced in advance every event that will happen and every move that's made, especially those by his enemies! In the end, there will be everlasting peace and order, beauty and rest, happiness and fulfillment — with no more pain, sickness, or sorrow (Rev. 19-22).

Between now and then, however, we've been entrusted with the greatest of all missions — the advancement of the kingdom of God. The essence of the kingdom is the rule and reign of the king in the lives of his people throughout the ages, from generation to generation until God closes time. Thus, after the king was installed, He commissioned His first followers to go and make disciples all over the world. That commission passes to every generation of disciples thereafter, to the end of the age.

What we need today is a *critical mass* of Spirit-empowered disciples from this generation — growing, multiplying, and changing the world for Jesus and the kingdom of God. J. Oswald Sanders was fond of saying that Christians have been called to nothing less than world conquest. But it's a conquest of grace, not of force. In theory, *critical mass* is the existence of sufficient momentum that becomes self-sustaining and fuels further growth. In a spiritual context, it involves the *personal spiritual growth* of individuals in all areas of maturity and *corporate spiritual multiplication* of the body of Christ through disciplemaking. These components — growing disciples, fruitful disciplemakers, and spiritual multiplication are the essential building blocks of the kingdom of God and the subject of this book. But let's begin with a discussion of the concept of *critical mass*.

The Jamestown Experiment

My earliest American ancestor was Joseph Cobb. In 1613 at age 25, he sailed for the "new world" and Jamestown, Virginia, on the *Treasurer*, commanded by Captain Samuel Argall.[1] Not long after his arrival, Argall, a famous sea captain, lured Pocahontas onto the ship and held her hostage on the *Treasurer* to broker a prisoner exchange and peace treaty with her father, Powhatan (Wahunsonacock), chief of the Powhatan Indian tribes. After she was freed, she stayed at the Jamestown fort and later converted to Christianity, married planter John Rolfe, and sailed back to England in 1614 to meet the queen on the same ship that brought my ancestor to America.[2]

At the time, the mortality rate in Jamestown was as high as 80 percent, and Cobb no doubt suffered many hardships, but he persevered, built a farm on 400 acres across the James River near present-day Smithfield, Virginia, and raised a family. His children and grandchildren multiplied and later migrated south and west. Now fourteen generations later, I'm one of a multitude of American descendants who claim Joseph Cobb as a direct forefather. But the rest of the story is that Jamestown almost failed three years before he arrived, and that could have changed everything!

In 2007 Jamestown celebrated the 400th anniversary of its founding in 1607, and even Queen Elizabeth II joined in the celebration. But we really can't imagine what life was like back then or how hard it was for those first colonists. Life was so bad and the mortality rate so high in those early years due to harsh weather and living conditions, internal and external conflict, disease, famine, and violence, that in 1610 every settler in Jamestown boarded the ships and headed down the James River to cross back over the ocean for home. They'd had enough and were abandoning Jamestown and the colonial experiment.[3]

They considered burning the settlement before they left, but decided not to bother. Before they cleared the mouth of the James River, they ran into the ship of Thomas West, Lord De La Warr, the new governor of the colony, sailing for Jamestown. He ordered them to turn around and go back. He brought fresh supplies and more people to help relieve their burdens and strengthen the colony. So despite their hardships and dwindling numbers, they went back, and though they continued to suffer innumerable hardships, they eventually succeeded and thrived.[4]

Today, hundreds of millions of Americans live in the "new world" as a result of the perseverance of those first colonists. What would have happened if they had abandoned Jamestown in 1610, three years after its founding in 1607? What if the colony had not reached critical mass? Well first, my ancestor Joseph Cobb may not have come to America. The settlement would have been abandoned. How might the future have been different? Would there have been subsequent attempts to colonize America? Spain was the dominant power of the day, and the Spanish had a tendency to kill or run off non-Spanish settlers in America. The Pilgrims didn't land at Plymouth (then considered Northern Virginia) until 1621, after and partially as a result of the fact that Jamestown became more stable. The Puritans of New England followed thereafter.

Without digressing into an argument over colonization, however, it's fair to conclude that the most successful and powerful nation in the history of the world to date came into existence as a result of the survival of Jamestown. The thirteen original colonies, the United States, and the Constitution all trace their ancestry to Jamestown. So because of Jamestown more than 400 years ago, America as we know it exists today. Jamestown almost failed, but eventually it reached *critical mass*, and the rest as they say is history.

Contexts of Critical Mass

The term "critical mass" is used in a variety of contexts — physics, chemistry, business, politics, and group dynamics.

It's simply a sustained chain reaction, which is a series of events so related to one another that each one initiates the next. In *group dynamics,* critical mass is a term that describes the existence of sufficient momentum that becomes self-sustaining and fuels further growth.[5] This definition presents three distinct elements of critical mass:

1. *initial momentum*
2. *sustained momentum*
3. *multiplied growth*

Progress and success are defined by the attainment of critical mass. And just as in a chemical or nuclear reaction, the failure to attain critical mass inevitably leads to decline. But where critical mass is attained, the movement or reaction takes on a life of its own and multiplies as a self-sustained chain reaction.

Jim Collins' bestseller *Good to Great* is an extensive analysis of critical mass in the business context. Though he doesn't use the term, he describes the transformational process of buildup to breakthrough, a framework wrapped around a concept he called the flywheel.[6] He summarized that everything in his book was an exploration and description of the pieces of the buildup-to-breakthrough flywheel pattern.[7]

> Sustainable transformations follow a predictable pattern of buildup and breakthrough. Like pushing on a giant, heavy flywheel, it takes a lot of effort to get the thing moving at all, but with persistent pushing in a consistent direction over a long period of time, the flywheel builds momentum, eventually hitting a point of breakthrough.[8]

He observed that at the point of breakthrough momentum kicks in to hurl the flywheel forward with an almost unstoppable momentum.[9] He concluded:

> Good to great comes about by a cumulative process—step by step, action by action, decision by decision, turn by turn of the flywheel—that adds up to sustained and spectacular results.[10]

I've exhausted my technical knowledge on the subject, so let me use the term in a popular sense. In describing a successful endeavor, we cite the time when goals were first achieved as the point of critical mass. Thereafter, success becomes contagious and the continued achievement and expansion of goals is multiplied over time. Let me give an example. My oldest son is a die-hard Boston Red Sox fan. For years, the Red Sox suffered under the so-called "curse of the Bambino," relating back to 1918 when Babe Ruth was traded to the Yankees and started their dynasty by winning the first of many World Series championships. In the interim, the Red Sox never won a World Series.

But in 2004, with the Yankees again leading in the ALCS three games to none, and six outs away from another World Series berth, the Red Sox came back to win the game, then three more games to claim their first ALCS victory over the Yankees, and then the World Series in a sweep of the Cardinals. They won a second World Series in 2007, and in those years were a regular contender. It took a while, but they finally hit critical mass.

I could tell numerous stories of mom-and-pop restaurants or businesses that struggled early but eventually grew, hit critical mass, and multiplied into national franchises. I could recount the traditions of champion football or basketball programs (like Notre Dame and UCLA) that rose to success after they found the winning combination of coaches, players, and strategies, coupled with hard work and perseverance, to reach a critical mass that lead to dynasties.

As I've considered these examples, I began to wonder if Scripture spoke to the concept of critical mass by analogy or otherwise. It's fitting we ask the question since spiritual issues are most important. So does the Bible speak of critical mass? Emphatically yes—it's everywhere! "For the earth will be filled with the knowledge of the glory of the LORD, as the waters cover the sea" (Hab. 2:14; Isaiah 11:9, NASB).

Critical Mass in Scripture

The very nature of the kingdom of God is, in the end, the greatest example of critical mass. Jesus described it like this:

> Again he said, 'What shall we say the kingdom of God is like, or what parable shall we use to describe it? It is like a mustard seed, which is the smallest seed you plant in the ground. Yet when planted, it grows and becomes the largest of all garden plants, with such big branches that the birds of the air can perch in its shade' (Mark 4:30-31, NIV).

He told them still another parable: 'The kingdom of heaven is like yeast that a woman took and mixed into a large amount of flour until it worked all through the dough' (Matt. 13:33, NIV).

One of the best examples of critical mass is found in Paul's *leadership multiplication model* in 2 Timothy 2:2:

- The things you've heard from me in the presence of many witnesses (*initial momentum*);
- Entrust to faithful men (*sustained momentum*);
- Who will be able to teach others also (*multiplied growth*).

17

Critical mass follows the momentum of the first leader's efforts and investment in a second generation of leaders, who raise up and invests in the third generation, who in turn reach the fourth. Timothy had seen Paul in action many times in many places, and was ready and well-trained to do the same himself. But Paul reminded him to seek out and invest in reliable leaders with the ability to teach others and keep the movement going. Timothy accepted the baton and fulfilled his own ministry. This verse illustrates the generational aspect of a genuine critical mass—*Paul, Timothy, faithful men, others also.* The initial momentum of Paul's ministry to Timothy became sustained momentum when Timothy reached and trained the next generation of faithful leaders, which fueled further growth in the generations after him.

In a spiritual context, it must be underscored that critical mass is induced and sustained *only* by the Spirit of God. I don't intend to suggest that man can stimulate and propagate a spiritual movement on his own. But notice the Spirit-led, multi-generational impact from life to life across time. I'm also not trying to set up a "Procrustean bed" as Tommy Nelson of Denton Bible Church describes it—form-fitting Scripture into a preconceived, man-centered philosophy (in this case a prescription for success), and lopping off the parts that don't fit. Likewise, I'm not addressing a particular eschatological position (pre, post, or amillennial view of end-times prophecy). And I sure don't want to start another Christian fad. However, by using the concept of critical mass as a creative stimulus, we can think outside the box to gain insight into God's intended plan for personal maturity and church growth through spiritual multiplication.

1 Thess. 1:2-10 illustrates the critical mass of Paul's *corporate multiplication model*:

- Our *gospel came to you* in word, power, the Holy Spirit, and deep conviction (v.5) (*initial momentum*).

- You know how *we lived among you* for your sake (v.5) (*initial momentum*).
- You became *imitators of us* and of the Lord (v.6) (*sustained momentum*).
- You became a *model to them* (v.7) (*multiplied growth*).
- The Lord's *message rang out from you everywhere* (v.8) (*multiplied growth*).
- Therefore, *we don't need to say anything* (v.8) (*critical mass achieved*).

Paul brought the gospel to the Thessalonians in all its fullness, but he and his staff also lived among them to model the Christian life. The Thessalonians imitated the lives of Paul and his men, so that the initial momentum became self-sustaining. Further growth was fueled when the Thessalonians became a model to others and the gospel rang out from them everywhere. Thus, spiritual-critical mass is a Spirit-driven chain reaction among people, progressing from *salvation* to *transformation* to *multiplication*.

This progression is poetically described in Isaiah 61:1-4, the beginning phase of which was cited by Jesus at the outset of his ministry in Luke 4:14-21. The Spirit anointed Jesus to bring the gospel to the poor, blind, broken-hearted prisoners. Liberty was proclaimed to the captives, freedom to the prisoners. There's an exchange, something for nothing — beauty for ashes, the oil of joy for mourning, the garland of praise for the spirit of heaviness. It's a picture of *salvation* by grace. As a result, the broken-hearted prisoners become oaks of righteousness, the planting of the Lord that He may be glorified — *transformation*. Then, the oaks rebuild the ancient ruins, the long-devastated society — *multiplication*. (*See also* Ezekiel 36: 10-11.)

Spiritual-Critical Mass

For my purposes, *critical mass* in a spiritual context consists of a two-fold process, both *personal* and *corporate*, that includes:

1. **Personal spiritual growth** in five main areas of spiritual maturity—*devotion, character, relationships, doctrine,* and *ministry*; and
2. **Corporate spiritual multiplication** as *citizen soldiers* (ordinary Christians) make *complete disciples.*

The spiritual version of critical mass boils down to the essential elements of *spiritual growth* and *spiritual multiplication.* The first is *personal,* the second is *corporate.* The first necessarily precedes, but is followed by, the second. Before we go any further, however, we must consider the source of all momentum and growth—God. A man-centered analysis is meaningless. Paul made it clear in 1 Corinthians 3:6-7 that he planted and Apollos watered, but God caused the growth or the increase. "So then neither the one who plants nor the one who waters is anything, but God who causes the growth (*or* gives the increase)" (1 Cor. 3:7, NASB). Critical mass was God's idea. Therefore, it's his process generated by his power. Let me give three examples.

First, Genesis 1:27-28 records that God created man in his own image—male and female (*personal*). Then he blessed them, and the first thing he said to them was to be fruitful, multiply, fill the earth, and subdue it (*corporate*). He individually created them in his own image, and from the beginning they were made in the likeness of God, with his qualities. They were holy; they were loving; they had the fruits of God's Spirit built into their character; they were relational; they knew truth; and they had a purpose. They were to multiply in kind—increase in number, fill the earth, and rule over it. God wanted many more in his image just like them. In fact, he wanted an entire planet-full of God-like ones living and thriving on the earth. As we know, things didn't turn out so well, and God eventually started over with Noah. But once again, after the flood in Genesis 9:1, 7, the first command from God to Noah was to be fruitful, multiply, fill the earth, and subdue it. His plan was still the same.

As a second example, recall that Abraham is the central figure of the book of Genesis and the patriarch of Israel. God changed his name from Abram to Abraham to signify that he would be the father of many nations. In Genesis 12 and again in Genesis 15, God made a covenant with him. He was 75 years old in Genesis 12 when God first promised to make a great nation of him. At that point, he had no sons, but God promised him innumerable descendants, and ultimately that all the nations of the earth would be blessed through him.

In Genesis 17, God repeated his promises to Abraham, who then was 99 years old and still waiting for the son of promise. Finally, at age 100, Isaac was born. From a human perspective, these promises weren't amounting to much. After 25 years and the best years of Abraham's life, he had only one promised son to show for it. We're picking up steam! If it were me, I'd have been discouraged or miffed. But God said to him, "Look up at the heavens and count the stars — if indeed you can count them. So shall your offspring be" (Gen. 15:5, NASB). Abraham believed God, and it was accounted to him as righteousness (Gen. 15:6).

Then again in Genesis 17:1-6, God said to Abraham:

> 'I am God Almighty; walk before Me and be blameless (*complete, perfect, having integrity*). I will establish My covenant between Me and you, and I will multiply you exceedingly. . . . And you will be the father of a multitude of nations. . . . I will make you exceedingly fruitful, and I will make nations of you. . .' (NASB).

Note God's concern for the integrity of Abraham's personal life along with the promise to multiply his descendants. Though Abraham didn't see the complete fulfillment, it did happen. Hundreds of years later, Moses said to the descendants of Abraham—the nation of Israel: "The LORD your God has multiplied you, and behold, you are this day like the stars of heaven in number" (Deut. 1:10, NASB).

Third, in Matthew 28:18-20 and Acts 1:8, Jesus pronounced his Great Commission. He began by stating that all authority in heaven and on earth had been given to him. The implications of that statement alone are profound. But from that ultimate source of power and authority, he commanded his disciples through the ages to be disciple makers in all the nations. He told them to start where they were, expand into the surrounding region, and ultimately to the ends of the earth. He instructed them to teach successive generations of disciples to obey and observe—that is to put into practice and live out everything he had taught his first disciples. This mission was paramount for his church and lasts to the end of the age. It was *personal* and *corporate*. It involved *spiritual growth* and *spiritual multiplication*. And most important, it originated with God and was empowered by God:

> Then Jesus came to them and said, 'All authority in heaven and earth has been given to me. Therefore go and make disciples of all nations, baptizing them in the name of the Father and of the Son and of the Holy Spirit, and teaching them to obey everything I have commanded you. And surely I am with you always, to the very end of the age' (Matt. 28:18-20, NIV).

> 'But you will receive power when the Holy Spirit comes on you; and you will be my

witnesses in Jerusalem, and in all Judea and Samaria, and to the ends of the earth' (Acts 1:8, NIV).

The Measure of Success

How then do we evaluate the efforts of the modern church in pursuit of its mission, and in what areas should we expect to see a critical mass? In other words, what is the measure of success? Many would say that success is measured by the size of the crowd in attendance—a packed auditorium. This standard applies across our culture. As a nation of consumers and spectators, size equals success and numbers lead to profit and popularity. That's why entertainers and athletes earn far more than anyone else. They draw the crowds. The American church has adopted the same mindset. Entertain and attract the crowds. Yet with larger crowds than any church in history, has the American church achieved a true critical mass?

The church today more resembles a college football game. On any fall Saturday, thousands of passionate fans gather to watch their team compete. Prominent universities have loyal followings and rich traditions. For example, the "twelfth man" tradition at Texas A&M began at a football game in 1922. Many of the players had been hurt by halftime, so the coach had to scour the stands for substitutes. E. King Gill was called on to suit up, and the tradition was born. Now, the entire student body is called the "twelfth man" for its passionate support of the team.

But unlike the original twelfth man, today there is absolutely no expectation that any fan will ever be called on to suit up and get in the game. They yell and support their team, but they're never more than spectators. And that's as it should be—it's a sport. Unfortunately, the American church has become like the twelfth man. We watch, but don't participate. We cheer, but stay off the field. In reality, the similarities between players and fans are minimal. Fans watch and cheer from a comfortable distance. Players get on the field and compete to win. They practice regularly, study the playbook, and take the hits. The only real similarity between players and fans are the colors they wear and the songs they sing.

In the church, there are far more fans than players, but is that by God's design? Jesus said that the harvest was plentiful, but the laborers were few (Matthew 9:37). But his point was that it shouldn't stay that way. "Therefore pray the Lord of the harvest to send out laborers into His harvest" (Matt. 9:38, NKJV). The church wasn't supposed to consist of a few players and a multitude of spectators, though it's much easier to be a spectator than a player. Even John Calvin faced this struggle. As he looked back over his career near the end of his life, he observed: "Being by nature a bit antisocial and shy, I always loved retirement and peace. . . But God has so whirled me around by various events that He has never let me rest anywhere, but in spite of my natural inclination, has thrust me into the limelight and made me 'get into the game,' as they say."[11]

Programs and Resources

Others would say that the measure of success is good programs and nice facilities. The quality of the programs and buildings determine the value of the ministry. But E. M. Bounds long ago commented on this position, stating:

> We are constantly on a stretch, if not a strain, to devise new methods, new plans, new organizations to advance the church and secure enlargement and efficiency for the gospel. This trend of the day has a tendency to lose sight of the man or sink the man in the plan or organization. God's plan is to make much of the man, far more of him than of anything else. *Men are*

> *God's method. The church is looking for better*
> *methods; God is looking for better men.*[12]

By analogy consider the D-Day invasion of France on June 6, 1944, the largest war-time operation in history. In one night and day, 175,000 fighting men and their equipment, including 50,000 vehicles, were transported over 60 to 100 miles of the English Channel and landed on hostile shore under intense opposition. The operation involved over 5,000 ships and crafts, and nearly 11,000 airplanes, and was in planning for over two years, involving the efforts of millions of people. It was equivalent to moving every man, woman, child, automobile, and truck from the Wisconsin cities of Green Bay, Racine, and Kenosha, to the east side of Lake Michigan in one night. Winston Churchill called it "the most difficult and complicated operation ever to take place."[13]

Yet for all of America's industrial brawn and organization, and for all of the plans and preparations, the *success or failure* of the invasion came down to a relatively small number of junior officers and enlisted men. To paraphrase Ambrose, if the paratroopers and other troops had cowered behind the hedgerows or hid in the barns, rather than seek out the enemy; if the coxswains had not driven their landing craft ashore in fear of enemy fire; if the men on the beaches had dug in behind the seawall; if the officers and noncoms had failed to lead their men over the seawall in the face of enemy fire, then the most thoroughly planned offensive in military history would have failed. But it didn't, and not because of firepower, machinery and weaponry. It succeeded because the troops believed in their cause and persevered in their mission. They were motivated, well-trained, and properly equipped—and the vast majority were *citizen soldiers*.[14] Remember that term!

Mature, fruitful disciples

Success in ministry is not measured by the size of the crowds or the quality of the programs and buildings. Success is not based on the speaking ability of the pastor, the quality of the music, or the presence of supernatural phenomena. Ministry success is measured by the *depth of maturity* and *quality of fruitfulness* in the lives of believers. Therefore, the main ministry of the church is to develop mature, fruitful disciples of Jesus Christ, and a top priority of the church is to train disciplemakers and spiritual leaders. By this the Father is glorified — that we bear much fruit, and so prove to be Jesus' disciples (John 15:8). This wasn't our idea; he chose us and appointed us to go and bear *lasting* fruit (John 15:16)!

In *The Lost Art of Disciple Making,* Leroy Eims posed the question: "Why are fruitful, dedicated, mature disciples so rare? The biggest reason is that all too often we have relied on programs and materials or some other thing to do the job. The ministry is to be carried on by people, not programs."[15] Mature disciples are not mass-produced, as Eims points out:

> We cannot drop people into a 'program' and see disciples emerge at the end of a production line. It takes time to make disciples. It takes individual, personal attention. It takes patience and understanding to teach them how to get into the Word of God for themselves, how to feed and nourish their souls, and by the power of the Holy Spirit how to apply the word to their lives. And it takes being an example to them of all of the above.[16]

The church is successful when it reaches critical mass, which is a two-fold process involving *personal spiritual growth* and *corporate spiritual multiplication*. On an individual level, *critical mass* is consistent personal growth in five main areas of spiritual maturity—an intimate walk with God; Christ-like character and fruits of the Spirit; strong relationships with people; sound biblical doctrine; and service and disciplemaking. Most every area of the Christian life will fit into one of these areas, and we need to grow continually in all of them. And we want to be balanced and complete, not lopsided and incomplete. As a body, *critical mass* is sustained corporate growth through the spiritual multiplication of the citizen soldiers in the church—the saints, the ordinary people —who make disciples everywhere they live and everywhere they go. And not just baby disciples or adolescent disciples, but mature, complete disciples—fully developed in every area of life.

A disciple is a learner, a student, a follower, and an imitator of another's life and lifestyle, priorities and values. In recounting the numerous revivals and movements from past church history, Tommy Nelson once observed that there had never been a movement or revival focused on equipping ordinary people in disciplemaking ministry. Revivals usually focus on salvation, but not on discipleship or spiritual multiplication. I'd like to see that movement in my lifetime, and I pray for a *critical mass* of *citizen soldiers* making *complete disciples* everywhere! The latter sections of this book focus on the two major components of **critical mass** in the church, **complete disciples** and **citizen soldiers**, but first I'll lay a foundation for discipleship and personal maturity.

2. Discipleship

*T*here are few Christian terms more familiar but less understood than *discipleship*. After years of neglect, discipleship appears to be a priority again, but the full experience of discipleship is the exception, rather than the norm. Our modern culture is partly to blame. Authentic discipleship should be central to the Christian life—but as a *way* of life, not just a body of knowledge. I'd like to discuss the basic premise of discipleship through several stories, a few from my own experience, some from the Apostle Peter's life, and some by historical analogy from the apprenticeship of Thomas Jefferson. I also want to compare and contrast the Greek and Hebrew views of education and knowledge to highlight the Hebraic concept of discipleship. Then I'd like to briefly tell the story of the modern father of discipleship, Dawson Trotman, founder of a discipleship ministry in 1933. Finally, I'll discuss the call to discipleship.

A New Center

Living in America, we tend to see God from a self-centered, prosperity-oriented perspective. After all, we have a divine right to success and happiness, right? It's in the Bible somewhere, or was that some other important document? At age 26, I didn't realize my worldview was constructed with me at the center and everything else, including God, in orbit around me. But God showed me pretty plainly that, in fact, he was the center of the universe, and that everything revolved around him. It's such a simple truth, but it took a major failure in my young life to learn it. And when I did, I began to understand the life of discipleship.

I went to law school to become a great lawyer, a worthy goal in my view at the time. I thought that if I asked for God's favor, he would make it happen. The step that guaranteed my road to success was selection as a member of the state moot court team, and later a major national team. My law school routinely won state and national moot court contests, beating more prominent law schools in appellate brief writing and oral argument competitions similar to debate. Law students who made these teams could write their ticket upon graduation and obtained invaluable skills as a lawyer. Our professor/coach was the top moot court coach in the country. So, to be trained by him was my singular goal in life at the time.

Only five people would be chosen for the next major team. I had already made a "farm team" in a lesser national competition, and was ready to be called up to the "bigs." You had one chance to impress the coach, and I was so confident in my abilities that I was sure to be the next ace for the team. So I went to his office and boldly asked for a chance to spar against his star national team as they were preparing for a big contest. He gave me a shot, but I was so nervous when I got up to argue before real courtroom judges that I performed poorly. But I still thought I had a good chance to make the next "varsity" team.

I remember the day the team names were posted for the next major contest on the law school bulletin board. I nervously went to read the list, only to find that my name was not on it. I didn't make the cut, and as a result, my moot court career was essentially over. I didn't realize it then, but I wasn't even in the running. I was devastated, and I even thought about quitting law school—there's no point finishing if I can't be the best. But most of all, I found that there was no pain like having your dreams crushed because you're simply *not* good enough.

That was the greatest failure of my life to that point, but it became the greatest blessing God could have given me. The course of my life changed forever because of what God showed me *after* that experience. I was a briefing clerk at a large law firm at the time, and I went back to my cub-hole office in shock after the team names were posted. In agony I asked God one question: "Was it your will?" That's all I had to know, and I didn't even need to know why at that point because my world was spinning out of control. My foundation had been shaken to its core. I'd acknowledged God in this pursuit, and he surely knew what it meant to me. How could this have happened? Everything had built up to this crucial point. Why didn't he help me succeed?

Then he impressed upon me clearly: "Yes, this failure was my will." And then he added: "Up to now you've been seeking your own glory, with me and everything else revolving around you. But life is about my glory, and *everything* revolves around me. Seek my glory — that's what life's really about!" It was as plain as if he was sitting there talking to me, though I heard no audible voice. It was like scales fell from my eyes, and I saw for the first time. "Seek *first* the kingdom of God" (Matt. 6:33). And that changed everything! I turned loose of my goals to follow hard after Christ, and be like him. I finished law school, but I never felt the same about it. It became my trade, not my life. Jesus became the driving passion of my life, and I was ready to follow a different course.

A New Direction

I'm just glad that no one's been following me around, writing down every rash thing I've done as an object lesson for everyone else! But that's why we love Peter. He's one of us. His experiences are not just anecdotal. They're typical of how many of us act in similar circumstances. Peter was an ordinary working man, a fisherman by trade, and a devout man, but the events recorded in Luke 5:1-11 changed the course of his life. Peter met Jesus some months before this episode near the Jordan River. He heard him preach and saw him perform miraculous acts (Luke 4:38-44). He'd also heard John the Baptist's testimony about Jesus (John 1:35-42). Jesus had even healed Peter's mother-in-law and stayed in his home. Peter had seen the crowds and heard the message before, but he was busy cleaning his fishing equipment the day Jesus borrowed his boat for a podium.

The fishing business was hard work, and Peter and his partners had nothing to show for an all-night effort. After finishing his talk and dismissing the crowd, Jesus told Peter to launch back into the lake for one more cast of the nets. Peter may have thought, "What does a carpenter know about fishing?" You fish at night because the fish feed near the surface in the cool of the evening. During the heat of the day, the fish swim in the deep part of the lake. But Jesus possessed an unusual authority. He could do things no one else could do, and his teaching cut to the heart.

Perhaps sarcastically, Peter reminded Jesus that he'd fished all night and caught nothing, but at his word they would try one more time. Then it happened—they caught more fish than they'd ever seen. Their nets began to break, and they called their partners James and John, and filled both boats till they began to sink. Now at this point, if Peter had been a typical self-centered American, he likely would have said: "We just found ourselves a new partner—a magic genie! We're gonna be rich! We'll need more boats, more men, and we'll need to franchise. This will be bigger than Bubba Gump shrimp!"

But that wasn't Peter's reaction, and it couldn't have been more opposite. Forget the fish and the greatest catch he'd ever seen. He was blown away and said, "Go away from me Lord; for I am a sinful man, O Lord!" (Luke 5:8,

NASB). And that was the right response! Peter reacted the same way all men do when they find themselves in the presence of deity. He suddenly became extremely aware of his personal sinfulness and inadequacy, coupled with a sense of overwhelming awe in the presence of divinity and holiness. Isaiah had the same reaction in the Lord's presence on the throne. "Woe is me for I am ruined! Because I am a man of unclean lips, and I live among a people of unclean lips; for my eyes have seen the King, the LORD of hosts" (Isaiah 6:5, NASB). John, the beloved disciple and closest friend of Jesus, had the same reaction in the presence of the glorified Christ. "When I saw him, I fell at his feet like a dead man" (Rev. 1:17, NASB).

Then Jesus lifted Peter's sights to something far greater than a prosperous business venture: "Do not fear, from now on you will be catching men" (Luke 5:10). His new mission would involve reaching and discipling men in advancing the kingdom of God! And with that, in a radical step of devotion, Peter and his partners, Andrew, James, and John, dropped their nets and left everything to follow him. What else takes priority? They entrusted their lives to Jesus and never looked back. This episode calls to mind Paul's radical statement of devotion to Jesus:

> But whatever was to my profit I now consider loss for the sake of Christ. What is more, I consider everything a loss compared to the surpassing greatness of knowing Christ Jesus my Lord, for whose sake I have lost all things. I consider them rubbish, that I may gain Christ. . . (Phil. 3:7-8, NIV).

Once you've seen this — once you've seen Jesus for who he is and what he's about, everything else pales, and all you want to do is follow him.

The Lost Art

That master trainer, Zorro (played by Sir Anthony Hopkins in *The Mask of Zorro*), understood that the most important quality of any disciple is teachability! A disciple is a learner, as he advised his apprentice and eventual successor (Antonio Banderas), stating: "There's an old saying, a very old saying: '*When the pupil is ready, the master will appear.*'"[17] In other words, when a person is hungry to learn, he becomes teachable and will submit to the training of a master. In fact, the Greek verb *matheteuo*, which is translated "make disciples" in the Great Commission from Matthew 28:19, means not only to *learn*, but to become *attached* to the teacher and become his follower in both doctrine and life conduct. This verb is distinguished from similar Greek verbs that simply mean to learn without any attachment to the teacher. Thus, a Christian disciple believes in Jesus and makes his teachings the basis of his life and conduct.[18]

But we need to get past our modern Greek notion of education, which today involves a teacher's monologue on a particular subject in a sterile classroom where students listen passively and take notes. The Hebrew concept of education was far richer. It certainly included classroom instruction, but it also involved extensive hands-on apprenticeship training. Alan Hirsch addressed these issues in his book, *The Forgotten Ways*. "The Hebrew worldview was a life-oriented one and was not primarily concerned with concepts and ideas *in themselves*." The Greeks, however, developed the disengaged and passive environment of the classroom.[19]

He noted the familiar gospel story "in which Jesus selected a band of disciples, lived and ministered with them, and mentored them on the road. It was the life-on-life phenomenon that facilitated the transfer of information and ideas into concrete situations." He observed that Jesus formed his disciples this way by design, and that authentic disciples are made no other way.[20] In diagnosing the cause for the state of modern discipleship, Hirsch insightfully wrote:

> How did we move so far from the ethos of discipleship passed on to us by the Lord? The cause lies in Western Christianity being so deeply influenced by Greek, or Hellenistic, ideas of knowledge. By the fourth century, in the church the Platonic worldview had almost triumphed over the Hebraic one. Later, it was Aristotle who became the predominant philosopher for the church. He too operated under a Hellenistic framework. Essentially a Hellenistic view of knowledge is concerned about concepts, ideas, and the nature of being. The Hebraic on the other hand, is primarily concerned with issues of concrete existence, obedience, life-oriented wisdom, and the interrelationship of all things under God. As Jews, Jesus and the early church quite clearly operated primarily out of a Hebraic understanding rather than a Hellenistic one.[21]

The problem we face, he observed, is that by merely addressing intellectual issues we're unable to change behavior. "The assumption in Hellenistic thinking is that if people get the right ideas, they will simply change their behavior." They won't, but the church largely follows the Greek model of education, which assumes that right thinking *alone* leads to right acting. The key to transforming lives, however, is found in the "ancient art of disciple making, which operates best with the Hebraic understanding of knowledge," and asserts that right acting leads to right thinking. Hirsch concludes that "[w]e need to take the whole person into account in seeking to transform an individual, and educate them in the context *of* life *for* life."[22]

A Traditional Apprenticeship

In addition, as society became industrialized and most everything became mass-produced, we also moved to a mass-production form of education and training. In earlier times, every trade or profession was learned through personal apprenticeship training. Discipleship operates on much the same premise, but it's foreign to most Christians today because of our modern culture. Let me illustrate the traditional apprenticeship process with an historical example. If you were asked to identify the most respected leaders from Virginia in 1776, you might name George Washington, Thomas Jefferson, or James Madison. But these men were still relatively young and unproven in 1776.

In the "class" of leaders ahead of these more famous founding fathers was George Wythe. In 1776 he was among the most respected men in Virginia. He was the senior delegate to the Continental Congress from Virginia in 1776. You may recall that the Declaration of Independence was signed at Independence Hall in Philadelphia — that is by most of the delegates. They brought the Declaration to George Wythe to sign at his home in Williamsburg, and they saved the top spot of the Virginia delegation's signatures for him. Next time you look at the Declaration, notice the block of signatures just below the prominent signature of John Hancock.[23]

George Wythe was a born teacher and the country's first law school professor at the College of William & Mary. The law school is partially named after him today. He was a man of many interests, including law, politics, science, and literature. He was a practicing attorney for many years, and you can still visit his home in historic Williamsburg. His office was in the back of the house on the first floor, and it was there he also apprenticed many a young law student. In colonial times, most young men entered their trade or profession after an apprenticeship, and this was true for lawyers as well.[24]

One especially bright, young student who trained under Wythe's tutelage was Thomas Jefferson. In fact, George Wythe was one of Jefferson's main heroes and mentors. For five years, Jefferson trained under George Wythe. Each morning, he walked from his rented room to Wythe's red-brick Georgian house on Palace Green in Williamsburg, and went to the back-room clerk's study. He read and studied the law using his master's extensive library, and was expected to observe closely each stage of every case in his master's office. Wythe taught Jefferson to treasure the morning and tackle the toughest readings early in the day. When Wythe traveled to outlying county courts, Jefferson rode with him.[25]

As Jefferson biographer Willard Sterne Randall documents:

> Wythe explained his every legal step to Jefferson and, as Jefferson progressed, Wythe gave him more and more responsibility for legal research in the provincial records and from Wythe's lawbooks, eventually turning over to him more of the out-of-court preparation vital for his master's clients. Under Wythe's watchful eyes, Jefferson learned law by handling actual cases. On court days in Williamsburg, Jefferson carried George Wythe's books and notes into the Palace for him and stayed nearby at his beck and call.[26]

Jefferson found that he and Wythe had many interests in common. In the evenings for example, Jefferson would often accompany Wythe to dinner at the Governor's Palace in Williamsburg, along with Wythe's close friends, Dr. William Small, Jefferson's college professor and earlier mentor, and the Royal Governor, Francis Fauquier. Jefferson would listen intently and join in their dinner discussions on a wide variety of topics, including literature, science, philosophy, and civics. From these discussions, Jefferson wrote that he heard and engaged in "more good sense, more rational and philosophical conversation than all my life besides." In later life he wrote, "to the habitual conversations on these occasions I owed much instruction."[27]

Jefferson called Wythe his second father, and rarely applied such terms of warmth to anyone, even his own parents. "He never tired of paying tribute to the 'beloved mentor' of his youth." In fact, he referred to Wythe as "My faithful and beloved mentor in youth and my most affectionate friend through life," and "My ancient master, my earliest and best friend." He considered it his good fortune to become acquainted early in life with a man of such high character and high standing, and wished to become the kind of man Wythe was. In trials and difficulties, he would often ask himself, "What would Mr. Wythe do in this situation?" As President, Jefferson looked back on the experiences of his early years and said, "I am indebted for first impressions which have had the most salutary influence on the course of my life." [28]

The fame of the protégé eventually exceeded that of his master. Among his many accomplishments, Jefferson authored the Declaration of Independence and the first Freedom of Religion Act. He and Wythe helped revise the laws of Virginia, which became the model for other states. He also designed our system of currency. While President, he doubled the size of the U. S. with the Louisiana purchase, and commissioned the Lewis & Clark expedition to explore the west. He was himself a mentor to other notable men, including James Madison, James Monroe, and Meriwether Lewis.[29]

Many years later when President Kennedy hosted a White House dinner for Nobel Prize winners, he was quoted as saying that they were "the most extraordinary collection of talent, of human knowledge, that has ever been gathered together at the White House, with the possible exception of when Thomas Jefferson dined alone."[30] Although I don't endorse certain of the spiritual beliefs of either Jefferson or Wythe, it's fair to conclude that Thomas Jefferson became a man of considerable influence, in large part, as a result of his training under George Wythe. And I use their example to illustrate the power and impact of apprenticeship. Incidentally, Wythe also trained other notable American leaders, including James Monroe, John Marshall, John Quincy Adams, and Henry Clay.[31]

The Modern Roots

The roots of modern discipleship can be traced to the Pietist movement of the late 17th century. As church historian, Bruce Shelley, observed: "Pietism arose as a reaction to [the] ossification of the Reformation," to challenge the nominal faith of German Lutheranism. Its purpose was two-fold. First, it stressed the importance of individual faith based on a believer's personal experience of God's grace. Second, it wanted to shift the center of Christian life away from state-sponsored churches towards intimate fellowships of active believers, who also spread the word of God to all classes of men.[32]

The first man to spearhead this movement was Philip Spener (1635-1705), a German Lutheran minister. Shocked by the spiritual condition of his first pastorate in Frankfort in about 1669, he began preaching repentance and discipleship. He later gathered a small company of dedicated believers to meet in his house regularly for Bible study, discussion, and spiritual development. "These meetings were soon called in scorn 'gatherings of the pious,' and 'pietism' was born." George Whitefield, John Wesley, and the Great Awakening in America arose from this movement.[33]

In the early-to-mid 20th century, modern discipleship took significant strides forward, starting with the ministry and leadership of Dawson Trotman (1906-1956), founder of a discipleship ministry called The Navigators. He is credited by many Christian leaders with bringing back into focus "foundational Bible truths which had been forgotten for years—the importance of personal follow-up of new

Christian converts, the one-to-one training of disciples, and the multiplication of disciples as a means of carrying out the Great Commission." Trotman was a man of contagious zeal, relentless drive, and unbounded creativity. He had a unique bi-focal vision for the salvation of the lost and the spiritual nurturing of a single individual.[34]

In 1933, his discipling ministry began in earnest with a young sailor named Les Spencer. Spencer came over for dinner one night, and afterwards the two took a drive into the Palos Verdes Hills, outside San Diego. They pulled over to talk about spiritual matters. Soon, however, a security guard from a nearby school pulled alongside the car, saw the Bible and the sailor, and was curious to find out what was going on. Before long the guard and Trotman were into a serious discussion of the Gospel and other Bible truths.[35]

Spencer watched in amazement as Trotman quoted and turned to numerous passages in answer to the guard's questions. On the way home Spencer told Daws that he would give his right arm if he could learn to do what he saw done that night. After testing his determination, Daws promised to teach him. They met regularly thereafter as Daws poured himself into Les' life, focusing on time in the word, prayer, evangelism, and follow-up. The next crucial step came as Daws began laying it on Les' heart to search for a man to disciple.[36]

It wasn't long before Les came to Daws excited about finding a hungry man, another sailor, Gurney Harris. He told Daws that he wanted to bring him over so Daws could train him the way he had Les. But Daws flatly refused, saying: "If you can't teach him what I've taught you, then I've failed." That profound statement marked a new era in the history of discipleship. *If you can't teach him what I've taught you, then I've failed.* By the end of World War II, Navigator ministries were on a thousand ships and scores of bases throughout the world.[37]

From this beginning, God used Dawson Trotman and the men he trained to build an international disciplemaking ministry that eventually reached more than 100 countries, and raised up generations of disciples around the world. Emphasizing a Christ-centered, Spirit-filled life, balanced in the word (quiet time, Bible study, Scripture memory and meditation), prayer, fellowship, and witnessing, along with in-depth follow-up of new disciples, and the training of laborers, Trotman's Navigator ministry grew and spread in military, civilian, and college environments.[38]

His emphasis on follow-up grew from his heart for evangelism, stating frequently: "You can lead a soul to Christ in from twenty minutes to a couple of hours. But it takes from twenty weeks to a couple of years to get him on the road to maturity."[39] At conferences, He would hammer home the importance of follow-up in the local church, once stating:

> What God wants are men and women born into His family who desire to be conformed to the image of His Son and to show forth the savor of His knowledge in every place. You lead a man to Christ. You tell him he's saved. You get him to join a church. You leave him. You let him go along living his former lifestyle. . . . Does it make sense? No; it doesn't make sense. You are in the greatest business on earth: that of bringing men and women into fellowship with Christ and to the place of greatest usefulness in God's marvelous plan. Your church is the heart and local headquarters of this tremendous program of taking the gospel of Christ to every creature and building in each believer a life that glorifies God. The worldwide success of this mission will be the giant reflection of its success in each community like yours.[40]

He longed to see every man a victorious, reproducing Christian. And one of his life mottoes was: "Never do anything that someone else can or will do, when there is so much to be done that others cannot or will not do." Investing in people, building lives, and discipling young believers top the list of ministries that most others cannot or will not do.[41]

Trotman drowned in a boating accident in June 1956. His close friend, Billy Graham, gave the message at his funeral at Glen Eyrie in Colorado. He described Daws as a great strategist and general, one who could look beyond handicaps, circumstances, and barriers in his efforts to reach and disciple people worldwide. Graham called him a man of vision and discipline, a man of the word and prayer, and a man of passion for people with eyes on eternity. But Graham said this about Trotman's single-minded devotion: "He was a man of *complete dedication*. He could say with Paul, '*This one thing I do*,' not 'These forty things I dabbled in.'"[42]

The Call

If you've made it this far, the rest of the book may not mean much to you if you haven't heard the call yourself. I've started to read many books only to chunk them after a few chapters when I don't connect with the story or when they don't hold my interest. If your reaction is the latter, please accept my apologies and chunk away. If you don't connect with the story, however, it may be that you don't know the Man, the God-Man, or I should say, Christ the King! For the fact remains that Jesus *is* the center of the story, and that's true whether you know it or not and whether you believe it or not. You can chase your own rainbows, but at the end of the day, there's really nothing there of lasting value. And the great irony is that no matter how strongly I say it, you won't get it unless you've heard the call yourself—unless you know Christ yourself.

The call is a revelation of how things really are, and an understanding of what truly matters. It's a revelation of the person of Christ, and a call to follow him. The Holy Spirit is entirely responsible for the call because his job is to reveal the truth about Jesus and about life (John 14:17, 26; 15:26; 16:8-14). Understanding the realities of sin, judgment, redemption, and faith are matters of personal experience. You see, it's the call that causes you to "drop the nets" to follow Jesus and get in the big game. After I heard the call, I asked myself, "Who do I know that lives like this?" An old college friend, George Black, came to mind, and by the hand of providence, he was moving to Houston where I was in law school. We met for the next year and a half until I graduated and moved away to take a job in Dallas. But in that time, he stoked my passion for Jesus and modeled a life centered on him in every way. George had a tremendous ministry to troubled youths, and his life had a huge impact on mine.

After I later moved to College Station to practice with a small law firm, I ran into another old college friend, Blake Purcell, who was just moving there to take over the college discipleship ministry of the Navigators at Texas A&M. I was looking for a ministry to get involved in, but didn't expect it to be with college students. Blake was such a charismatic leader with a highly focused vision for discipleship that I was drawn to his ministry. I wanted to be a part of what he did. I met with him for the next four years and worked in his ministry. I had never known anyone with such a finely tuned philosophy of ministry and discipleship. He understood spiritual development and maturity, as well as disciple making and spiritual multiplication. I watched and helped, and grew immensely myself. Then one day he felt called to leave and start the first discipleship ministry located in St. Petersburg, Russia, and left the A&M ministry to me.

Afterwards, I gained a clear conviction that I wanted to maintain a fruitful disciplemaking ministry from the platform of a tentmaker. God didn't call me into full-time vocational ministry, although I seriously considered it on more than one occasion. Thus, in order to live as a tentmaker and serve as a disciplemaker, I had to live a *fully integrated lifestyle.*[43] The four main areas of my life—*personal, family, work,* and *ministry,* had to be coordinated and balanced or the "tyranny of the urgent" would dictate my priorities and neutralize my effectiveness. In other words, I had to figure out how to manage my personal life, love my wife, raise my kids, go to work, and invest in a few men. There were costs to count, but his grace was sufficient.

3. *Teleios*

I remember the first time I heard the question. I was at a missions conference in College Station in the 1980's. The speaker was Dr. Earl Radmacher, then president of Western Seminary in Oregon. He asked if we could describe the goal of the Christian life in one word. One word, are you kidding? I'm a lawyer—I can't say anything in one word! How can you summarize the goal of the Christian life in one word? He was trying to get us to focus. Several years later, the man who became my long-time discipler and mentor, Ford Madison, asked the same question at a ministry workshop: "In a word, what is the goal of the Christian life?" His answer was the same as Dr. Radmacher's — *Christlikeness*. The ultimate goal is simply to become like Christ in every area of life. Jesus said that a disciple when fully trained will be like his teacher (Luke 6:40). Paul said that God's destiny for us is to be conformed to the likeness of his son (Rom. 8:29). Our old lives were crucified with him, and he now lives in us (Gal. 2:20). Thus, we were positionally *complete* in Christ the moment we were saved, but we still need to *mature* as disciples (*see* Heb. 10:14).

Mature—Complete

My favorite Greek word in the New Testament is *teleios*. Not that I'm a Greek scholar, but as an attorney I'm a trained professional at faking expertise on any subject!

Even so, I think this term is so important that it warrants a chapter. *Teleios* means *complete, mature, perfect,* or *finished.* Depending on your Bible translation, one of these four words is used to interpret *teleios* as an adjective or its two main derivatives as a verb (*teleioo* and *teleo*). It appears in the New Testament 19 times as an adjective and 51 times as a verb, and reveals much about the nature and scope of Christlikeness.[44] In fact, I'll say that it's the single best term to describe Christlikeness.

Teleios means to be fully developed in every area of life, not just some areas. It means to be whole, of full stature, fully grown, and having all the necessary parts. The person is not a novice, a child, or an adolescent. As a verb, the term means to reach a definite goal and finish the course well.[45] Jesus commands us to become *perfect* (*mature, complete*), just as our Father in heaven is already *perfect* (Matt. 5:48).

Paul was confident that God would *complete* the work he began in us (Phil. 1:6). Paul pursued *perfection* (*maturity, completion*) as his personal goal with the vigor of a Greek athlete, and said that all *mature* people had this attitude (Phil. 3:12-15). Paul's ministry goal was to present every person *complete* (*mature, perfect*) in Christ (Col. 1:28-29). He said that the church's ministry goal was to build a unified body of *complete* (*mature*) disciples (Eph. 4:11-13). Paul concluded his last letter by stating that he had *finished* (*completed*) his course, kept the faith, and won the victor's crown (2 Tim. 4:7). I'm beginning to see a pattern here:

o Jesus calls us to be **complete** like the Father (Matt. 5:48).
o God **completes** the work he began in us (Phil. 1:6).
o Paul pursued **completeness** as the goal of his own life (Phil. 3:12-15).
o Paul's ministry goal was to develop **complete** disciples (Col. 1:28-29).
o The church's ministry goal is to build a unified body of **complete** disciples (Eph. 4:11-13).
o Paul **completed** his race and won the prize (2 Tim. 4:7-8).

The Mission Statement

I stumbled on this all-important word while studying Paul's mission statement in Col. 1:28-29. Nowhere does he more succinctly state his ministry purpose than here:

> We proclaim Him, admonishing every man and teaching every man with all wisdom, so that we may present every man *complete* in Christ. For this purpose also I labor, striving according to His power, which mightily works within me (Col. 1:28-29, NASB, *emphasis added*).

The laser focus of Paul's ministry was to develop *complete* disciples. Considering all that Paul did to establish the church, this statement spotlights his ultimate goal. Remember that Paul wrote much of the New Testament, articulating the major doctrines of the Christian faith. He planted and shepherded numerous churches, training many of their leaders. But he never lost sight of the forest for the trees. "Toward this goal I also labor," the NET Bible says (Col. 1:29, NET). His ministry was focused on the full development of *people*. You don't see Paul elaborate on the details of programs, materials, or facilities. Contrast that today with much of the focus on the quality of our *stuff*. But what of the people who use or supposedly benefit from the stuff? How are they doing? What do their lives look like? Are they maturing in their attitudes and actions, their faith and character? Do we see new generations of disciples rising up through the influence of their lives? Or do the buildings just get bigger, the programs more polished, and the meetings more entertaining?

Churches and ministries often engage in a flurry of activity, but with limited productivity or focus. Their programs look good on paper and run efficiently, but do they effectively develop the lasting fruit that glorifies God (*see*

John 15:8, 16)? In reality, many churches are lopsided. They are strong in emphasizing some areas of the Christian life, but weak in others. They develop spiritual growth in some areas, and neglect others. Churches and ministries have temperaments like people do, and depending on their bents, they have different strengths and weaknesses. Some churches emphasize relationships. Others emphasize doctrine. Some emphasize missions, and others community. Some focus on teaching, others on worship. All of these are important, so the real challenge is to model and promote a mature and well-rounded spiritual life.

Part of the problem comes from our limited view of education, as discussed in the previous chapter. Paul said that in proclaiming Christ, he admonished and taught everyone so that they would become complete in Christ. This was the central purpose of his ministry—to present everyone complete or mature in Christ. All his efforts were focused and directed toward this ultimate goal. In a positional sense, these believers were made complete in Christ upon their salvation, but they still had to grow up in the faith and become who they were destined to be! They were born into the royal family, but they still had to grow to maturity. How then were they taught to become who they are?

The biblical view of education and training is more akin to the modern role of coaching. Football coaches begin by teaching the plays to their players using a playbook and chalkboard. The players learn the plays through a conceptual understanding of their individual and corporate roles and movements. It takes a fair amount of energy to mentally learn the plays, but they're just getting started. Likewise in ministry, classroom learning is the first step, but too often we see it as the only step.

After the players learn the plays, the coaches take them out to the field and practice running the plays over and over again, day in and day out. The coaches run individual and team drills for the players to learn their various positions, and each week the team practices the plays they'll use in the game. But not until the team can execute those plays in a live game where the score counts and the team wins have the coaches successfully coached. Training complete disciples should be the same. Not until they can live out the Christian life in the real world have we taught them to be mature disciples. And the job will stretch us to the end of our means and take all the spiritual energy God provides (Col. 1:29)!

The Life Race

Yet Paul's ministry goal was no different than his own personal goal, and he pursued it with the passion and commitment of an Olympic athlete.

> Not that I have already obtained it or have already become *perfect* (*complete, mature*), but I press on so that I may lay hold of that for which also I was laid hold of by Christ Jesus. Brethren, I do not regard myself as having laid hold of it yet; but one thing I do: forgetting what lies behind and reaching forward to what lies ahead, I press on toward the goal for the prize of the upward call of God in Christ Jesus. Let us therefore, as many as are *perfect* (*complete, mature*), have this attitude (Phil. 3:12-15a, NASB);

Paul was fond of using athletic imagery to illustrate the normal Christian life of discipleship (*see also* 1 Cor. 9:24-27; 2 Tim. 2:5; Heb. 12:1-2). He knew he hadn't arrived, but he was ever pressing forward to the goal set for him by Christ—to be complete—to become like Christ in every area of life. And he encouraged other disciples to have the same mindset.

This passage raises an interesting question. What exactly did Paul mean that he was training like an athlete—and training for what? Was it just an attitude or something more? He made it plain a few verses later. "Join with others in following my example, brothers, and take note of those who *live* according to the pattern we gave you (Phil. 3:17, NIV)." *Life* was the race he was running. "Do you not know that those who run in a race all run, but only one receives the prize? Run in such a way that you may win (1 Cor. 9:24, NASB)." Live the Christian life to *win*! Do you realize how great that challenge is and how great the reward is? It's one thing to win a big race after strenuous training, as hard as that is, but it's an altogether different experience to win at *life*!

Life is far more important, and at the same time, far more involved and complex. We all know athletes who win championships, but fail terribly at life. We know businessmen who succeed beyond their wildest dreams, but lose their families in the process. I want to win at *life* — and I mean every part of life, life as a whole, life in total — not just a sport, a job, or some isolated event. I want to win at every meaningful and eternal part of life, and God wants that too! He's empowered us to do just that — to his glory. It's the normal Christian life. There's no greater race, no greater challenge, and yet few seem to win, but it should not and need not be so!

This Greek word for "win" is an interesting term — *katalambano*. It means to obtain, to attain, to lay hold of, and to grasp.[46] So in Phil. 3:12-15, Paul was saying that he had not yet won, nor was he complete, but he pressed on to the goal to win the prize. He's alluding to the Olympic Games in his eager and strenuous exertion to win the greatest prize. The Greek word for "race" also refers to the Greek games. *Agon* was a place of contest, a stadium, or a race course. It refers to a contest for victory used in the Greek games of running, boxing, and wrestling. In the New Testament, it was used to illustrate the life task of the Christian.[47] Our word "agonize" derives from this term. Finally, the Greek term for "run," *trecho*, figuratively refers to the Greek games in describing the Christian's strenuous efforts in the Christian life and cause.[48]

Let me then paraphrase 1 Corinthians 9:24. Everyone knows that all the runners in a race run for the finish line, but only one wins the race. Live the Christian life like the winner of a race! The point is not to suggest that only a few can win at living the Christian life. Rather, the point is to motivate and challenge every Christian to be a winner at life! Impossible you say? Right you are. The Christian life is impossible, but Colossians 1:29 illustrates the key: "For this purpose also I labor, striving (*agonizing*) according to His *power*, which mightily works within me." The power of God's Spirit mightily works through my agonized labor to live the Christian life and advance the cause of Christ. The Spirit's power enables life and service, but it's something of a paradox. I agonize in exerting strenuous effort in the race, empowered by God to run and win!

It's been done many times before. In fact, there's a hall of fame of winners who still inspire today. As a result, we were challenged by the writer of Hebrews to lay aside the weights that slow us down—the good things that keep us from the best things, and the sin that so easily ensnares us and knocks us out of the race, and run with endurance the race set before us (Heb. 12:1-2). Jesus did it; the great heroes of the faith did it; and we can do it too! Do you want to say like Paul at the end of your life that you fought the good fight, finished the race, and kept the faith (2 Tim. 4:7)? Do you want to claim the victor's crown laid up for winners (2 Tim. 4:8)? I sure do!

The Complete Disciple

So let's ask the next question—what does it take to win and what exactly are we training for? In other words, what is a *complete* disciple? Is maturity a subjective concept? They say that beauty is in the eye of the beholder. Is it the same for maturity? You know it when you see it, but it's difficult to describe, and everyone sees it a little different. No, maturity is not an existential experience. You don't make up your own version. God has designed it as the crown jewel of his beautiful creation, the very reflection of His likeness formed in man.

Paul said he labored to present everyone complete in Christ, but what did he mean? What was he building into their lives? In his own life, Paul pressed on to Christlike maturity. It was the same goal. But what are the traits or characteristics of a mature, complete Christian? Let's start by thinking in terms of a blueprint. No one builds a house without a blueprint, and it must include all essential components, including foundation, plumbing, framing, roof, walls, insulation, electric wiring, etc. The details of each component must be properly designed and constructed, but the overall blueprint keeps the builder on track with the finished project in view.

Figure 1 is my blueprint of a *Complete Disciple*. It includes the essential traits and characteristics of a mature Christian as revealed in Scripture. The key components include: ***devotion***, ***character***, ***relationships***, ***doctrine***, and ***ministry***. These are broad headings that represent what I consider to be the five main areas of the Christian life, discussed at length in the next section of this book. I can fit most every aspect of life into one of these five areas. They reflect the essential priorities of the Great Commandment, the Great Commission, biblical truth, and personal holiness.

There are, of course, many ways you could depict and describe a mature follower of Christ, and I invite you to design your own version. Mine is simply offered to illustrate a profile reflecting the major areas of growth and development in a Christian's life. A blueprint or profile helps bring into focus the purpose and goal of ministry. How can we know what we're building if we don't have a blueprint? My home church chose to use a mature oak tree to illustrate the five key areas of growth and maturity. The root system is composed of *devotion* and *doctrine*. The trunk is *character*, and the crown includes *relationships* and *ministry*. The oak tree also serves as an excellent means of communicating the major aspects of spiritual maturity (*see* Psalm 1:3; Isaiah 61:3; Jer. 17:7-8).

THE COMPLETE DISCIPLE
BLUEPRINT

Devotion

◊ Grace and faith
◊ Love and obedience
◊ The Word and prayer

(Col. 1:28-29)

Character

◊ Christ-centered
◊ Fruits of the Spirit   **Doctrine**
◊ Holiness

Relationships

◊ Family
◊ Friends
◊ Community

◊ Authority of Scripture
◊ Law and grace
◊ Essential theology

Ministry

◊ Vocation/Profession
◊ Spiritual gifts and service
◊ Disciplemaking

Figure 1

Devotion is the first and foremost area because it involves a person's relationship with Christ, which is the foundation of the Christian life. This most important of relationships is established by the grace of God through faith in the finished work of Christ on the cross, dying in our place for our sins. The Great Commandment underscores that love for God is first priority. Once established, an intimate relationship with Jesus is nurtured by obedience, which is life lived out in response to the will of God. Regular time in the word and prayer are the primary means of fostering a relationship with Christ and facilitating personal spiritual growth. (*See for example*: Matt. 22:36-40; John 14:21, 23, 15:4-5, 7-8; Rom. 5:8, 6:23; 2 Cor. 5:17; Eph. 2:8-9; Col 3:16.)

Character is the second main area of the Christian life—a life that is increasingly Christ-centered and less self-centered, a life that honestly addresses areas of sin and cultivates the fruits of the Spirit—love, joy, peace, patience, kindness, goodness, faithfulness, gentleness, and self-control. In other words, it involves the life-long process of putting off the old fleshly life and putting on the new spiritual life. And it involves holiness in every part of life. (*See for example*: Matt 5:48, 10:38-39; Rom. 12:1-2, 13:14; Gal. 5:22-23; Eph. 4:20-24; Col. 3:5-10; 1 Peter 1:14-16.)

Relationships comprise the third main area of the Christian life, and the second half of the Great Commandment to love your neighbor as yourself. Your closest neighbors are your family, friends, and community. And if relationships are the fabric of life, then wives, husbands, children, friends, church, and local community comprise its primary weave. The best evidence for the truth and credibility of Christianity to the outside world is the way in which Christians love and relate to each other. (*See for example*: John 13:34-35, 15:12-13, 17; 1 Cor. 13:4-7; Col. 3:18-21; Heb. 10:24-25; 1 John 4:7-11.)

Doctrine is the fourth major area. A Christian is under the authority of Scripture, not the other way around. A thorough understanding of the biblical doctrines of law and grace that characterize the Old Testament and the New

Testament is vital to the formation of an accurate world-view and theological paradigm. Every believer must be grounded in essential and primary theology — those foundational beliefs that distinguish the Christian faith from all other belief systems. These include the truth and inerrancy of Scripture; the Trinity; the deity of Christ; the role of the Holy Spirit; the incarnation, crucifixion, and resurrection; salvation and judgment; heaven and hell; and other primary doctrines. (*See for example*: 1 Tim. 4:6; 2 Tim. 2:15, 3:14-17, 4:3-4; Titus 1:9; Heb. 5:12-14.)

Ministry is the final area of the Christian life. Every Christian is gifted and called to ministry of some type. A person's vocation or profession will be one such place of ministry. God has ordained certain spiritual gifts and spheres of service, including stewardship (financial giving), for all his children in the building up the body of Christ. In particular, Jesus called his followers everywhere and in every generation to win the lost and disciple the saved. We've been given the high privilege of advancing the kingdom of God — inspiring and investing in the next generation of Christian disciples, laborers, and leaders. (*See for example*: Matt. 28:18-20; John 13:13-14; Acts 1:8; 1 Cor. 12:4-7; 2 Cor. 9:7-8; 1 Thess. 2:7-12; 2 Tim. 2:2.)

Church Ministry Dynamics

How then are complete disciples made? How do they develop? The church, the local body of believers living in community, is the primary environment God created to nurture his children to maturity. The three venues of *large group* (church services, conferences, retreats), *small group* (Sunday school, cell groups, Bible studies, men's and women's groups), and *life-to-life* (one-to-one discipling and mentoring relationships), facilitate the development of God's people. The leaders and professionals of the church utilize these venues to equip the ordinary people of the church, the citizen soldiers, to carry out the ministry of making complete disciples.

Perhaps the best explanation of church ministry dynamics is found in Ephesians 4:11-13:

> And He gave some as apostles, and some as prophets, and some as evangelists, and some as pastors and teachers, for the equipping of the saints for the work of service (*ministry*), to the building up of the body of Christ; until we all attain to the unity of the faith, and of the knowledge of the Son of God, to a mature (*teleios*) man, to the measure of the stature which belongs to the fullness of Christ (NASB).

The NET Bible says "to equip the saints for the work of ministry, that is, to build up the body of Christ, until we all attain to the unity of the faith and the knowledge of the Son of God—a mature (*teleios*) person, attaining to the measure of Christ's full stature." (Eph. 4:12-13, NET). The Amplified Version says in verse 12 that "His intention was the perfecting and full equipping of the saints (His consecrated people), [that they should do] the work of ministering toward building up Christ's body (the church)" (Eph. 4:12, Amp.).

This passage shows that:

- *Jesus* raises up leaders of various gifting and function.
- *Leaders* equip the saints to do the work of ministry.
- *The Saints* (God's people—the *citizen soldiers*) do the work of the ministry.
- The *ministry* is building up the body of Christ in corporate unity and personal maturity.

That's the essential mission of the church! Spiritual leaders train ordinary lay Christian ministers or laborers to make disciples and help them grow to maturity or completeness. Note the expansive *"teleios"* theme throughout this passage from verses 13 through 16: "a mature person"

(v. 13), "the measure of Christ's full stature" (v. 13), "no longer children" (v. 14), "grow up in every way (in all aspects)" (v. 15), and "causes the growth of the body" (v. 16). Can it really be that simple? *Leaders equip laborers to make complete disciples!* The essence of *critical mass* in the church is that leaders (*initial momentum*) train laborers (*sustained momentum*) to make complete disciples (*multiplied growth*). And the body builds itself up in Christ!

Leaders equip *laborers* to make *complete disciples*. How have we managed to garble this straight-forward mission so badly over the years? I've read that few pastors can articulate a vision for their church, and a large percentage of churches have either plateaued or are dying.[49] It need not be so! Summarizing the lesson of Ephesians 4:12, the old Wycliffe Bible Commentary emphasized:

> That is, it is the business of all the saints — not of a few leaders only — to carry on the work of the ministry. The leaders are for the purpose of perfecting or equipping believers to carry on this work. Most local churches today do not follow this NT idea. It is common practice to let the pastor do the ministering. Sometimes the pastor temporarily may find it easier to do the work himself than to train others to do it. But his job is to train up workers, and in the long run his ministry will be more effective if he does so.[50]

The next section of the book discusses in more detail the five major areas of the *complete disciple*. The final section discusses the church's *citizen soldiers* who live as *tentmakers* and serve as *laborers* (disciplemakers). It then addresses the role of *pathfinders* (spiritual leaders) in providing ministry training, and the legacy of *patriarchs* through spiritual multiplication across generations.

II.

Complete Disciples

4. Devotion

*O*swald Chambers said it well: "Discipleship means personal, passionate *devotion* to a Person, Our Lord Jesus Christ. There is a difference between devotion to a Person and devotion to principles or to a cause. Our Lord never proclaimed a cause; He proclaimed personal devotion to himself."[51] Our first love is always Jesus himself, and we have difficulty keeping this priority straight. Just ask the Ephesians who felt the rebuke of Jesus' personal message to them in Revelation 2. These believers were commended for their commitment to principles and the cause, but rebuked for the loss of their first love. They seemed to have abandoned the priority of the Great Commandment, to love God with all their heart, soul, mind and strength (Matt. 22:36-40; Mark 12:28-30).

I doubt they had to be reminded of their first love early in their spiritual life. It was supernaturally instinctive to their new life in Christ. It was exhilarating, fresh, and vibrant. But over time, *the principles* and *the cause* took precedence. Why do we do that? Now don't distance yourself from those Ephesians! We've all done this. A. W. Tozer rightly said: "To have found God and still to pursue Him is the soul's paradox of love, scorned indeed by the too-easily-satisfied religionist, but justified in happy experience by the children of the burning heart."[52]

But the first point to remember is that God pursued us first! We love Jesus because he first loved us and made the ultimate sacrifice to accomplish our rescue (1 John 4:10). Our devotion to him is a responsive love born initially from our gratitude for an unearned gift of immense value – the saving of our lives. And there is higher motivation still. Jesus possesses a glory superior to anything in the universe. He is awesome and awe-inspiring! He is majestic and fascinating. He has no rival and no competition, and yet he cares for the least of us. He has the qualities of both goodness and greatness, traits not always found in the same person. He is supreme, and *because of who he is*, he's worthy of our highest devotion.

I can't begin to cover all there is to say on this topic, but I'll address three important aspects of our devotion to God. The first and foremost is *grace and faith*. Our relationship with Christ is based entirely on his grace operating through faith. Apart from the grace of God extended to us without merit, we would not know God, much less have a relationship with him. Instead, we would be lost eternally in our sin. The second aspect of devotion involves *love and obedience*. God loves us and commands us to love him with our whole being – in heart attitude and obedient action. Our relationship with Christ is based and built on *agape* love – an honoring and unconditional love that seeks the highest good of another. The third part of devotion addresses the primacy of *the word and prayer*. These two comprise the means of cultivating a relationship with Christ. God has communicated his truths and purposes in his word. We give him praise, seek his guidance, and rely on him through prayer.

Grace and Faith

We live in a performance-oriented society. Although we support equal opportunity, we don't all achieve equal results. At our best, we excel on our merits; at our worst, we rise on social or political connections. In either case, it's what you achieve or who you know that leads to acceptance and success. You've either earned your way or someone else let you in on their coat tails. That's why we have a hard time with the concept of *grace* because neither of these means of advancement carries weight with God.

We can't possibly achieve enough to gain his acceptance, and there is no one with the social or political connections to get us into his kingdom. We're unfit and rejected outright, and we just can't live with that result. And so, we try to change the rules, as though God were subject to our control. Remember the age-old evangelism question: "If you were to stand before God and he asked you why he should let you into his kingdom, what would you say?" Many would say that they've been pretty good most of their lives, certainly good enough to earn a spot in heaven. Oh really? As my old law professor used to say, "is that based on karma or some credible authority?"

To understand grace, we must begin with an understanding of sin and judgment. Grace seems cheap indeed without the proper context. Grace is unmerited and unearned favor. As a result of sin, however, what you've earned is judgment, punishment, exile, and death. And yes, you have sinned, "for all have sinned and fall short of the glory of God" (Rom. 3:23, NASB). No one can credibly dispute their imperfections and failings. But it gets better; "the wages of sin is death" (Rom. 6:23, NASB).

On your own, there's no way out. You cannot escape your sentence, no exceptions. Your sin, and I mean *your* sin, has earned you God's just and eternal punishment, banishment, and condemnation. Nothing *you* can do by your own efforts will change it, and you're hopelessly naïve to think your good points will somehow outweigh your bad. God is the master of the universe and he alone sets the standard of righteousness and perfection. If you don't measure up, and *you* most assuredly do not, then you're rejected. And it's ridiculous to believe that people are basically good. They're not. They're fundamentally corrupt.

Then there's hell. We don't like to think about it, especially in our modern society. But hell is a very real place, just as real as every maximum-security prison, full of hardened criminals. In God's eyes, you are a criminal and therefore his enemy. You will not escape, whether you ignore reality or run from it. And however bad you think it is on earth, you have no idea what awaits you for all eternity. I honestly can't bear to think about it. But I do know that life is short, eternity is not!

Unless you get to a place of hopelessness due to your circumstances, you cannot understand grace. As much as you might try to deny or avoid it, you are guilty, and your penalty is far harsher than you can possibly imagine. At this point, the Triune God intervenes by stepping down from his judge's bench, taking off his black robe, and putting on your hideous orange prison garb. You are set free with no criminal record while he is lead off to the chamber to face the execution scheduled for you. He dies and you go free. The judge becomes the prisoner, and the prisoner is pardoned. There had to be justice and there had to be an execution for your crime, and it makes absolutely no sense that the judge himself would submit to the punishment meant for you, but he did!

The grace you were shown was motivated by an unconditional love that reveals the most extraordinary part of his nature. "Very rarely will anyone die for a righteous man, though for a good man someone might possibly dare to die. But God demonstrates his own love for us in this: While we were still sinners, Christ died for us" (Rom. 5:7-8, NIV). We were in fact his enemies when he reconciled us through the death of his son (Rom. 5:10). But it was the love of God that moved him to show you grace. Imagine that—the criminal becomes a child! Who else acts like this?

This most precious of gifts, however, is received one way and only one way. "For it is by grace you have been saved, through faith—and this not from yourselves, it is the gift of God—not by works, so that no one can boast" (Eph. 2:8-9, NIV). Faith is the sole bridge to freedom. It's also the primary means of relational connection with God. "And without faith it is impossible to please God, because anyone who comes to him must believe that he exists and that he rewards those who earnestly seek him" (Heb. 11:6, NIV).

As Hebrews 11 describes, the men of old were commended for their faith (Heb. 11:2). They lived and died by faith, and despite the fact that they had use of their five senses, their lives were guided by that intangible sense of faith in the living God. If the Scriptures and the godly men of past ages teach us anything, it is that faith is the indispensable means of encountering God, obtaining his favor, and restoring the relationship he intended that we enjoy with him. Faith, therefore, is the assurance of the things we hope for and the conviction of the things we presently don't see (Heb. 11:1). We're saved by faith in the finished work of Christ, and we live by faith in Christ, who loved us and died for us (Gal. 2:20).

So you must ask yourself: Have you come to know Christ in a personal way, and put your trust in his sacrifice on the cross to resolve the problem of your sin? If you have, you are saved from the penalty of sin—eternal punishment and separation, and you will be welcomed into God's eternal home as a much-beloved child. And by faith, his intended relational connection is re-established. Consider the profound reality that the immortal, infinite God of the universe wants to relate to *you*! It's almost unfathomable. Who am I that God would care to know my name, much less relate to me? What can I possibly offer him? But he loves *me* and wants me to know him and follow his son.

Love and Obedience

In trusting Jesus for the forgiveness of sin, you became a new creation and established a love relationship with the Triune God. As a result, you are able to experience uninterrupted fellowship and communion with God. The presence of the Holy Spirit within you enables such relationship. Consider for a moment the father heart of God and his unconditional love and acceptance! We have a hard time grasping the true nature of unconditional love because it's so rare and so foreign to our understanding.

God loves because it's part of his essential nature to love, not because there's something worthy or attractive within the object of his love. The natural love of man, on the other hand, is *object-based*. There's something about the loved one that attracts or earns such love, either physical beauty, some characteristic of value, or earned respect. We offer God none of these qualities to merit or attract his love. His love, instead, is *nature-based*. It flows from the nature of his being to extend love to people, and has nothing to do with the qualities of the loved ones. In fact, we are at the outset quite ugly and unattractive to him. There's no good reason he should love us based on our innate qualities or worth. But he accepts us without qualification on the basis of Jesus' perfect qualifications.

To what then shall we compare the love of God? Consider the intimate love of a nursing mother for her newborn baby. Is it possible for a mother to forget her own child? Not likely. Yet God described his own love for us by asking that very question. "Can a woman forget her nursing child and have no compassion on the son of her womb? Even these may forget, but I will not forget you" (Isaiah 49:15, NASB). The Scriptures hold many such descriptions of God's intimate and sacrificing love for his children. "It was I who taught Ephraim to walk, taking them by the arms; but they did not realize it was I who healed them. I led them with cords of human kindness, with ties of love; I lifted the yoke from their neck and bent down to feed them" (Hosea 11:3-4, NIV).

God's unconditional love cannot be earned, and therefore it cannot be lost. Once having entered the household of faith, the Father does not reject his children. He will discipline his children for disobedience, but he will never leave them nor forsake them (Heb. 12:7-8, 13:5). God's love for us never changes, but we might draw a distinction between *acceptance* and *intimacy*. On the basis of Jesus' finished work on the cross, God accepts us unconditionally by faith. Intimacy, however, is cultivated through consistent fellowship and communion with God. The Holy Spirit was given to accomplish this very purpose (John 14:16-17, 15:26).

But intimacy is also contingent on obedience. While God's *acceptance* is unconditional on the basis of faith, our depth of *intimacy* with God is conditioned on holiness that follows obedience. Jesus said: "He who has My commandments and keeps them is the one who loves Me; and he who loves Me will be loved by My Father, and I will love him and disclose Myself to him" (John 14:21, NASB). We show our love for Jesus through our obedience to his commands. He went on to say: "If anyone loves Me, he will keep My word; and the Father will love him, and We will come to him and make our abode [home] with him" (John 14:23, NASB). Our level of intimacy with Christ flows directly from our obedience to his word.

Yet, obedience is a term we struggle with in the modern world. We tend to equate obedience with legalism, but it's not legalism! We wrongly think of obedience as forced behavior against our will as an external show of loyalty to gain or retain acceptance. That's legalism, but not obedience. True obedience is the outward manifestation of an inner reality. We are obedient when we *put into practice* and *live out* the truth we believe. Devoted love shows itself through obedience. Abraham believed God and it was credited to him as righteousness (Rom. 4:3, James 4:23). But as James points out, he showed that he believed God by his actions (James 2:21-23). He lived out his faith and because of his obedience, Abraham enjoyed the highest of intimacy with God who promised him countless descendants and blessing to all nations through his seed, Jesus (Gen. 22:11-18).

Our *attitude* of love for God is expressed in our *actions* of obedience. Such love is not primarily an emotion or feeling, but an action and a way of life. Feelings may, of course, follow or accompany action or behavior. But the true evidence of love is obedient action or behavior, not feelings or emotion. The great men and women of God express their love for God by their *daily walk of obedience*. Adam and Eve's disobedience broke their intimacy with God. As God walked in the garden in the cool of day, he noticed that they had hidden themselves (Gen 3:8-9). Before then, they likely accompanied him on these sunset walks and enjoyed intimate fellowship.

After the fall, Genesis 5 describes the descendants of Adam and Eve by how long they lived, except for Enoch. He's described by how long he *walked* with God. Then one day God simply took him home (Gen 5:22-24). His was a truly unique relationship, and Enoch is only one of two people who didn't face death. A few generations later, Noah was described as a righteous man who *walked* with God (Gen. 6:9). His life was blameless in a world of corruption. His obedience literally set him apart (along with his family). Everyone else drowned!

The Word and Prayer

God implants within us a hunger to know him and pursue him. If we feed the hunger, it grows. If we neglect it, it pales. Among the greatest of truths is that God may be cultivated. J. Oswald Sanders was fond of saying that you are as close to God as you choose to be, not as you wish to be. God yearns for us to seek him and then reveal himself to us. If we seek him, we will find him (Luke 11:9-13). The prophet Hosea exhorted: "So let us know, let us press on to know the LORD. His going forth is as certain as the dawn; and He will come to us like the rain, like the spring rain watering the earth." (Hosea 6:3, NASB.)

The primary means of relating to God and learning his ways is through his word. The Bible is the indispensable and necessary staple of the Christian life, and without a regular intake of the word, our spiritual lives are anemic at best. All Scripture is God-breathed, that is—the very word of God, and all Scripture is profitable for our growth (2 Tim. 3:16). The Bible is useful for instruction, rebuke, correction, and training so that we may be complete and thoroughly equipped for every good work (2 Tim 3:16-17). God's word leads us in the right direction, and if we get off track, it rebukes and corrects us. It trains us in righteousness.

There are five ways we can take in the word, and we should avail ourselves of all five. Just as your hand has five fingers and with them you can grasp of an object, so too by exercising the five means of taking in the Bible we can develop a strong grasp of the word of God.[53] These five include: *listen, read, study, memorize,* and *meditate.* I can *listen* to someone else share the word in a church service or at a retreat or conference. I can *read* the Bible in my quiet time or devotional time. I can *study* the Bible through a variety of book studies, and inductive or deductive studies. I can also *memorize* the word using the Topical Memory System or other method, or simply write down important or meaningful verses on the back of my old business cards.

If these four are the fingers of a hand, then the opposable thumb is *meditation.* I can meditate on what I hear; I can meditate on what I read and study; and I can meditate on what I memorize. And if I avail myself of these means of taking in the word of God, then I can develop a strong and steady grasp of its truths, and God can mold my life, strengthen my walk, and deepen my relationship with him. These spiritual disciplines should become as regular and normal in our lives as eating and drinking, such that we thrive on their presence and hunger at their absence. "How sweet are your words to my taste, sweeter than honey to my mouth!" (Psalm 119:103, NIV.)

When it comes to quiet times or devotional times, in particular, I'm a firm believer in taking in the whole counsel of the word of God on a regular, yearly or bi-yearly basis, from Genesis to Revelation. I've also found that yearly Bible reading plans are useful to pace me in such effort. We tend to camp on those portions of the Bible that are most meaningful or inspiring to us, but God intended us to take in the whole counsel of his word, including the "broccoli" and "spinach" parts of the Bible. They too give us meaningful insight and instruction into the character and work of God.

If daily quiet times are a refreshing rain, then Bible study is a deep soaking of the tap roots. Whether from New Testament book studies or Old Testament character studies, your insight into all things spiritual, your relationship with Jesus, and your life itself are transformed through regular Bible study. Scripture memory adds another dimension to your walk with God. While memorization itself can be taxing, think of it as downloading software. You can't do anything with it unless it's stored on your hardware. But once the word of God is *hidden in your heart* (Psalm 119:11), the Holy Spirit will use it many ways in your life! Remember that "the word of God is living and active and sharper than any two-edged sword, and piercing as far as the division of soul and spirit, of both joints and marrow, and able to judge the thoughts and intentions of the heart" (Heb. 4:12, NASB).

Prayer, on the other hand, appears something of a paradox. God already knows what I'm going to say before I say it; he knows what I need before I ask. So why pray? Surely it's more than a required ritual. And who am I that God would listen to anything I have to say? Yet, if we consider the *five means* of engaging the word as *one hand*, then the *other hand* is made up of the *five modes* of prayer. These include *praise & thanksgiving, confession, provision, intercession,* and *guidance*. But prayer begins with *praise & thanksgiving* to God for all that he is and all he's done:

> Great is the LORD, and highly to be praised,
> And His greatness is unsearchable.
> One generation shall praise Your works to another,
> And shall declare Your mighty acts.
> On the glorious splendor of Your majesty,
> And on Your wondrous works, I will meditate.
> (Psalm 145:3-5, NASB.)

When we praise and thank God for who he is and what he's done, it calibrates our focus and adjusts our perspective. But more important, he is *worthy*, and for this reason we were created — to offer him praise and thanksgiving.

Praise the LORD!
Praise, O servants of the LORD,
Praise the name of the LORD!
Blessed be the name of the LORD
From this time forth and forever.
From the rising of the sun to its setting
The name of the LORD is to be praised.
(Psalm 113:1-3, NASB.)

It is no small privilege to enter the presence of God and speak to him directly through prayer. In Jesus name, we have direct and immediate access to the great and eternal God of the universe, and we don't have to go through another intermediary to reach him. But with great respect and reverence, and because he is good and merciful and true, we should be careful to:

Enter His gates with thanksgiving,
And His courts with praise.
Be thankful to Him, and bless His name.
For the LORD is good;
His mercy is everlasting,
And His truth endures to all generations.
(Psalm 100:3-4, NKJV.)

Likewise, in order to cultivate an honest and transparent relationship with the Lord, we regularly confess our sins and seek his forgiveness. He already knows, but *confession* maintains the intimacy of our connectedness to God as we repent — that is agree with his view of our sin, and turn from it. For he is faithful to forgive and cleanse us from all unrighteousness (1 John 1:9). We also remember that God alone is our provider, not our employer, not our talents, not our savings, only God. We seek his *provision* for all our needs, from the most basic—food, shelter, and clothing, to the most complex—career, health, and family relationships. Our God supplies all our needs according to his glorious riches in Christ (Phil. 4:19)!

Intercession is prayer offered for others—the pleading or mediation in prayer for other people. I can relate to this concept because I do the same as a lawyer. I plead to the court as an advocate on behalf of my client seeking the power of judicial authority to enforce legal rights or redress wrongs suffered. In fact, Jesus is our advocate before the Father, the *paraclete* who intercedes on our behalf (1 John 2:1). The Holy Spirit is also described by Jesus as our *paraclete* because he comes along side to help us, comfort us, and counsel us (John 14:16, 26). And the Holy Spirit intercedes on our behalf with groanings too deep for words (Rom. 8:26). So likewise, we pray for the needs of others, identify with their pain or loss, and beseech God to help them in their need and glorify himself in their weakness.

God cares about the problems that arise in our lives, and uses them for our ultimate good and his glory (Rom. 8:28). But God is proactively working in the world to advance his kingdom and the reign of his son, the one-and-only king. He beckons us to do the same as the first priority of our lives (Matt. 6:33). He's far more interested in fulfilling the Great Commission than we can imagine (Matt 28:19-20)! Therefore, we seek his *guidance* to find our place of service and ministry as part of his overarching plan to rescue and redeem his lost children, and to build them up to maturity and fruitfulness in Christ. Jesus said that he only did what he saw the Father doing (John 5:19). He sought and submitted to the guidance of the Father in directing the course of his life and personal activities. Jesus also challenged us to ask great things of God and expect him to answer! (John 14:13-14, 15:7, 16:23-24.) His promises are incredibly great and far-reaching, but our prayers are often puny and short-sited.

Lorne Sanny, the long-time president of the Navigators after Dawson Trotman, was fond of sharing his personal approach to seeking the Lord's guidance on various ministry issues and the weighty problems he faced around the world.[54] He began in prayer by reciting Psalm 5:3: "In the morning, O LORD, you hear my voice; in the morning I lay my requests before you and wait in expectation" (NIV). He brought every problem or circumstance to the Lord in his prayers, leaving them with him, surrendering himself, and waiting expectantly for God's answer. He acknowledged that God was sufficient to answer these prayers on his own, in his time and as he willed, but Lorne made himself available to take whatever action God may direct as part of the answer. He simply asked that God prompt him or give him an idea as to what action he should take.

5. Character

*Y*our *character* is the most valuable thing you own, and the only thing you *truly* own because it's the only thing you'll take with you into the next life. Everything else stays here when you die, and that makes everything else a perishable item. The only imperishable thing you own is your *character*. So what's it worth? Well that depends on its purity, just like any precious metal or gem. At times, this present life operates as a purifying oven, though we don't like the heat. But God is far more interested in our holiness than our happiness.

We'll be happy for all eternity, and experience much happiness now, but God is presently more concerned with our holiness as he transforms us into the likeness of his son. He wants us to be like Jesus in every respect, and every fruit of the Spirit is an aspect of Jesus' character — love, joy, peace, patience, kindness, goodness, faithfulness, gentleness, and self-control. Conversely, "those who are Christ's have crucified the flesh with its passions and desires" (Gal. 5:24, NASB). Chief among them are pride, lust, anger, and greed. A person's character, therefore, is comprised of his attitudes and actions.

Christ-centered

My grandfather, John Evans, served in the Marine Corps in China during World War II. When he returned, he concluded that mankind's single greatest problem was selfishness. Men are entirely selfish by nature, and all human woes find their origin in this primary trait—selfishness or self-centeredness. Man is desperately egocentric in his fallen state. Even after his redemption, he battles his stubbornly self-centered flesh for the remainder of his natural life.

Jesus addressed this death-to-self struggle as a fundamental prerequisite to a fruitful spiritual life. Paul heavily focused on this same battle in his letters to the churches. Thus, in order to understand the nature of true Christ-centeredness, we must comprehend the depth of our natural self-centeredness. The odious self-life has carefully camouflaged itself so that we don't often recognize it. It's such a comfortable part of who we are that we can't imagine living without it. However, unless the self-life is exposed and dealt with, it remains a fatal cancer and the lens or matrix through which we view all of life, and that to our peril. Innate self-centeredness is the most deceptive and yet familiar part of our natural lives.

To be centered on Christ necessarily means that you are no longer centered on yourself. To be centered on Christ is to regard others with equal or greater value. And there can be only one center of your life, and either Jesus, you, or some other idol will occupy it. Everything else flows from the center—your values, priorities, and perspectives. In describing the second half of the Great Commandment, Jesus said that we should love others the way we already love ourselves. I naturally love myself, but it was a radical concept to love others the same way. The Golden Rule teaches us to treat others the same way we want to be treated because we don't naturally do that. We look out for our own interests first, and may not care about anyone else. But Paul said: "Do nothing from selfishness or empty conceit, but with humility of mind regard one another as more important than yourselves; do not merely look out for your own personal interests, but also for the interests of others" (Phil. 2:4-5, NASB).

When a person places his faith in Christ, he becomes a new creation with a new center (2 Cor. 5:17). The old disposition of complete self-centeredness passes away and everything in life becomes new and reborn, with a new disposition and a new center. Apart from rebirth, a person remains hopelessly egocentric. After rebirth, everything changes, and Jesus becomes the leading influence in life. Now a person is able to escape the vanity of a self-centered life and live for the glory of God. The old self-life loses it absolute control, but still retains the power to influence through old habits.

There can be only one king on the throne of your life. Jesus is the rightful sovereign, but the natural self has rebelled and made itself ruler, disrupting the original order of life. In one of the most repeated statements in the Gospels, Jesus makes abundantly clear the absolute prerequisite for discipleship — denial of self:

> Then he said to them all: "If anyone would come after me, he must deny himself and take up his cross daily and follow me. For whoever wants to save his life will lose it, but whoever loses his life for me will save it. What good is it for a man to gain the whole world, and yet lose or forfeit his very self?" (Luke 9:23-25, NIV.)

A version of this statement is repeated no less than six times in the Gospels (*see* Matt. 10:38-39, 16:24-26; Mark 8:34-36; Luke 9:23-25, 17:33; John 12:25-26).

Jesus presents the ultimate paradox: the one who finds his life will lose it, but the one who loses his life will find it. In other words, the one who seeks his fame and fortune in this life, chasing the proverbial gold at the end of the rainbow, will see it all vanish. And in fact, the person who lives a self-centered life focused on this present world loses out twice. First, he dies and loses it all when this life comes to an end. Then, in a far greater loss, he misses out on the blessings of eternal life with God. The distinguished commentator, Dr. William Barclay, wrote:

> There is no place for a policy of safety first in the Christian life. The man who seeks first ease and comfort and security and the fulfillment of personal ambition may well get all these things—but he will not be a happy man; for he was sent into this world to serve God and his fellow-men. A man can hoard life, if he wishes to do so. But that way he will lose all that makes life valuable to others and worth living for himself. The way to serve others, the way to fulfill God's purpose for us, the way to true happiness is to spend life selflessly, for only thus will we find life, here and hereafter.[55]

You can hoard life for yourself, or you can spend it for others and the kingdom. You can jealously guard all that you've garnered in this life, or you can freely use it to bless others and glorify God. You can love this world and all that it temporarily offers, or you can love the things of God, the things of eternal value. Take Demas for example. He started well as a trusted member of Paul's ministry team, mentioned more than once as part of the esteemed company that included Luke, Epaphras, Aristarchus, and Mark (Col. 4:14, Phlem. 24). But by the time Second Timothy was written several years later, Demas had deserted Paul because he loved *this present world* (2 Tim. 4:10).

Timothy, however, was another story. He was one of a kind. Despite his apparent weaknesses, Paul gave him the highest commendation a Christian servant and leader can receive when he said of Timothy:

I have no one else like him, who takes a genuine interest in your welfare. For everyone
else looks out for his own interests, not those
of Jesus Christ. But you know that Timothy
has proved himself, because as a son with his
father he has served with me in the work of
the gospel (Phil. 2: 19-22, NIV).

Timothy was neither double-minded nor half-hearted. He
was faithful and committed. He genuinely cared for the
welfare of others—the things of Jesus, the things of the
kingdom. He was not wrapped up in his own interests, and
his life is still a great testimony today. Timothy was a man of
proven character, both in attitude and action.

Fruits of the Spirit

Spiritual fruit is the product of a Christ-centered life,
cultivated as a normal part of spiritual growth and maturity. But it all depends on the "abiding." Jesus made clear in
John 15 that if we abide in him and his word abides in us,
we *will* bear fruit, and not just temporary fruit, but *lasting*
fruit! We cannot bear such fruit of ourselves, but only as we
abide in the true vine of Jesus. This metaphor of vines and
fruit paints a picture of complete dependence on the Spirit
of God to produce in us the fruit of righteousness that has
real and lasting value. Our responsibility is to abide in him,
remain in him, trust in him, draw our life from him, and rely
on him exclusively in all aspects of life. He then produces
the fruit. By this the Father is most glorified—through the
fruit borne in our lives. This wasn't our idea; it was all his
(*see* John 15:4-5, 7-8, 16).

And a high ideal it is, but how does it manifest in our
lives? How do we get beyond abstract theory and live it
out? In other words, what does it mean to abide? John uses
the Greek term *meno* (translated abide or remain) 11 times in
chapter 15, 40 times in his entire gospel, and 27 more times in

his epistles. It's a key word in John's theology. To abide is to be, and remain, united with Jesus in heart, mind, and will.[56] It means to be in close and settled union.[57] To abide is to cultivate a relationship with him, to continue in his teaching, and to continue in service to him. Of course, abiding begins with accepting Jesus as savior, but it also means to persevere in faith and loving obedience.[58] No lasting fruit is produced without it.

Regular time in the word and prayer are central to abiding in Christ. The older I get, the more convinced I am that the simplest things are the most profound. Nothing shapes, recalibrates, and transforms my attitudes and actions more than daily time in the word and prayer. From Genesis to Revelation on a regular basis, I remain committed to reading, studying, and meditating on the truths of the Bible. There is no substitute, and I'll say that there is no abiding apart from regular time in the word and prayer — listening to God, talking to God, interacting, relating, following, and living it out.

Spiritual fruit, therefore, is the certain byproduct of abiding in the vine. But what is the fruit? Initially, it includes the whole character of a person, that which motivates and directs his attitudes and actions. These are succinctly described as the nine fruits of the Spirit in Galatians 5:22: *love, joy, peace, patience, kindness, goodness, faithfulness, gentleness,* and *self-control.* These fruits describe the central attributes of Jesus himself, the traits that the Spirit wants to inculcate in our lives. They don't grow naturally in our lives. Quite the opposite! Apart from Christ, our lives are full of pride, lust, anger, greed, and all manner of selfishness. We mask civility and gracious behavior in social settings to portray a certain persona, but in our heart of hearts we are corrupt — apart from Christ.

Let's take a closer look at these nine spiritual fruits. The first three fruits are attitudes of the heart and mind. *Love, agape*-love, is the greatest of these, and the singular defining characteristic of a Christian. Love is unselfish and self-sacrificing. It seeks the highest good of others, even at great personal cost. (More on *agape*-love in Chapter 6.) *Joy* is a state of happiness not dependent on temporary circumstances, but on a relationship with Christ. Joy is anchored to the eternal state. No matter the present circumstances, joy remains and invigorates. *Peace* is the inner repose and calmness of spirit, even in the face of adverse circumstances. It defies human understanding because it comes from God. Peace also describes the harmonious relationships between people.[59]

The second three fruits involve our actions toward others. *Patience*, or longsuffering, refers to the willingness to endure inconvenience or injury by others and to accept irritating or painful situations. Patience is the quality of forbearance under provocation. It does not retaliate when wrongfully treated. *Kindness* is the tender concern for others, reflected in the same gentle treatment by which the Lord treated us. It is benevolence of action toward people such as God demonstrated toward sinners. It is good-hearted, gracious behavior. *Goodness* is moral and spiritual excellence that shows itself in active kindness to others. It is an uprightness of soul that does good to others even if undeserved. And it is beneficial in its effect.[60]

The next three fruits guide the general conduct of believers. *Faithfulness* is the quality that makes a person reliable or trustworthy. It is loyalty to a person and commitment to a task. Faithfulness is consistent conduct inspired by faith. *Gentleness*, or meekness, marks a person who is submissive to the word of God. It is patient submission in every offense, with no thought of revenge. Gentleness is also considerate of another when discipline is needed. *Self-control* refers to the restraint of fleshly passions and appetites. It denotes self-mastery and the curbing of selfish impulses. This virtue prevents bad conduct, while the other eight promote good conduct.[61]

This list of character qualities is certainly not exhaustive (*see* Col. 3:12-15; Eph. 4:2). Three more spiritual fruits that bear mentioning include *compassion, humility* and *integrity*, bringing our total to twelve. **Compassion** is an unusually touching expression, referring to tender sympathy and concern for others. It means to have pity, to suffer with, and to seek to relieve another's pain. God's compassion never fails, and Jesus often expressed an attitude of compassion toward others (Lam. 3:22; Matt. 9:36). **Humility** is the trait that allows one to give preference to others, and consider others better than himself. It's the opposite of pride, where one considers himself better than others. Humility does not demand undue self-deprecation, but rather lowliness of self-estimation and freedom from vanity. **Integrity** is honesty and consistency in all things and in all circumstances. A concrete foundation supporting a house lacks integrity if it has a crack or defect that compromises the consistency or stability of the slab. Often used in the Old Testament, it means completeness (*see* 1 Kings 9:4; Ps. 78:72).[62]

As with any fruit-bearing tree, the fruit itself is evidence of the maturity of the tree, and in our case, the maturity of our character. The second characteristic of fruit, however, is the seed of new life. A tree reproduces and multiplies as a result of its fruit. This second of the two-fold nature of fruit is addressed in some detail in Chapters 9-12 as part of the discussion on the ministry of ordinary people in the church. In fact, each of these two qualities of spiritual fruit occurs as a result of the critical mass discussed in Chapter 1—a critical mass of *personal spiritual growth* and *corporate spiritual multiplication*.

Holiness

Holiness is the culmination of spiritually-mature character. To be Christlike is to be holy. "[B]ut like the Holy One who called you, be holy yourselves also in all your behavior; because it is written, 'You shall be holy for I am holy'" (1 Peter 1:15-16, NASB). Holiness is a familiar term, but often without depth of understanding. To be holy is to be separate from the common condition; to be sanctified, sacred, pure, and without sin; sharing in God's purity, while abstaining from earth's defilement. In particular, it means to be perfect and without blemish (Rom. 12:1).[63]

The first word that describes God is "holy." And holiness is not just one of God's many attributes, but the one word that calls attention to *all* that God is. His love is holy; his justice is holy; his mercy is holy; his knowledge is holy; his word is holy.[64] His Spirit's only title is the "Holy" Spirit. And while God is love, the only source of *agape*-love, his Spirit is not called the Loving Spirit but the Holy Spirit. Therefore, we may conclude that God's first and highest quality is holiness, and that should give us pause for reflection. R. C. Sproul said:

> The primary meaning of *holy* is 'separate.' It comes from an ancient word that meant, 'to cut,' or 'to separate.' Perhaps even more accurate would be the phrase 'a cut above something.' When we find a garment or another piece of merchandise that is outstanding, that has a superior excellence, we use the expression that it is 'a cut above the rest.'
>
> When the Bible calls God holy it means primarily that God is transcendentally separate. He is so far above and beyond us that He seems almost totally foreign to us. To be holy is to be 'other,' to be different in a special way. The same basic meaning is used when the word *holy* is applied to earthly things.[65]

Because God is holy, his people are called to be holy — consecrated to God and set apart (or distinct) from the world.

> For I am the LORD your God. Consecrate
> yourselves therefore, and be holy, for I am
> holy (Lev. 11:44, NASB).

The children of Israel were a consecrated people, not merely in the sense of being God's inheritance as a special people, but by separating themselves from the abominations of the heathen nations around them.[66]

> Speak to all the congregation of Israel and
> say to them, 'You shall be holy, for I the LORD
> your God am holy' (Lev. 19:2, NASB).

The church is likewise called to be holy. God saved us and called us to a holy life, not because of anything we've done, but because of his own purpose and grace (2 Tim. 1:9). In view of God's incredible mercy, the Apostle Paul urged us to offer our bodies as a living and holy sacrifice in a spiritual act of worship (Rom. 12:1). In other words, we're to offer our whole lives to God. Paul then instructed us not to be *conformed* to the world's values, but to be *transformed* by the renewing of our minds in order to live out God's good, pleasing, and perfect will (Rom. 12:2).

Paul's use of the contrasting terms *conform* and *transform* reveals an important insight into the life of holiness. By nature, people will conform to their surroundings and the values of the prevailing culture. The Bible exposes this pattern of behavior time and again. The nation of Israel was continually warned against mingling with the surrounding heathen nations and learning their sinful ways (Psalm 106:35). Yet, they did it over and over again. It's human nature. We want to indulge the senses and appetites. We also want to be popular and progressive. We want to fit in and get along. We follow the latest trends and fads. We conform. And when society's values change, or they would say "evolve," we re-conform!

Your college philosophy class taught that *truth* is relative, and that each generation must decide for itself what is truth. In a rough application of the Hegelian dialectic, the prevailing culture or *thesis* of a generation is a blend of the values, priorities, and ideologies of the day. At the same time, there exists a contradictory and perhaps minority view that forms the *antithesis* of society. Over time, the conflict between the two is reconciled through compromise in the next generation, which forms a new *synthesis*. This succeeding generation is enlightened and progressive, having determined its own relative truth.[67] And who doesn't want to be at the forefront of evolutionary change? So we conform, and so it goes!

Or does it really go anywhere? Man's behavior, and therefore his history, tends to repeat itself. King Solomon wisely said:

> A generation goes and a generation comes. . .
> That which has been is that which will be,
> and that which has been done is that which
> will be done. So there is nothing new under
> the sun (Eccl. 1:4, 9, NASB).

Nevertheless, by nature we conform to worldly values no matter how enlightened we think we've become! By employing an unusual Greek word for "conform" in Romans 12:2, Paul exhorts us not to shape our lives to meet the fleeting fashions of this world, nor be like a chameleon that takes its color from its surroundings. Instead, be transformed from it![68] As another commentator has said:

> The ideas conveyed by the terms used to
> express nonconformity and transformation
> are striking. The first has the root *schema*,
> implying external semblance; the other is
> derived from *morphe*, meaning essential
> and radical likeness. . . . The consequence is

the recognition of God's will as right and fit and ideal.[69]

Transformation involves a total change from the inside out as a continual process. From the Greek word for "transformed," we derive the English word "metamorphosis." The essential man changes from a self-centered life to a Christ-centered life. Key to this change is the mind, or the control center of a person's attitudes and actions. As a result of continuing spiritual input of the word and prayer, along with Christian fellowship, service, and outreach ministry, a person's life is transformed by the Spirit to be more and more like Christ's.[70]

> And we, who with unveiled faces all reflect the Lord's glory, are being transformed into his likeness with ever-increasing glory, which comes from the Lord, who is the Spirit (2 Cor. 3:18, NIV).

Paul made the same argument in Ephesians and Colossians using the imagery of *putting off* old clothing and *putting on* new clothing (Eph. 4:22-24; Col. 3:5-10). The old self, or the old nature, is corrupted by all manner of sinful desires and actions, while the new self, or the new nature, is created to be like God in holiness. Paul tells us to strip away and take off the old, filthy clothes, and put on new clothes of a different quality and nature.[71]

> You were taught, with regard to your former way of life, to put off your old self, which is being corrupted by its deceitful desires; to be made new in the attitudes of your minds; and to put on the new self, created to be like God in true righteousness and holiness (Eph. 4:22-24, NIV).

One commentator observed:

> Grace, as nature, abhors a vacuum. To divest oneself of evil habits is not enough; this must be followed by the donning of the new nature, imparted at the new birth by the Spirit and to be increasingly recognized as the dominant moral force in the Christian's life as he faces an inner conflict.[72]

In more stark language, Paul exhorts that we actively put to death whatever belongs to the earthly or sinful nature (Col. 3:5; Rom. 8:13). This seems like an impossible task given the strength of our sinful desires under the old nature. And it is! Only through the Spirit's enabling power can we lay aside the old ways and walk in the new ones. If we walk in the Spirit's power, we won't carry out the desires of the sinful nature (Gal. 5:16). As Christians, we now have the power to choose—walk in the old life or walk in the new. And old habits die hard! "But put on the Lord Jesus Christ, and make no provision for the flesh in regard to its lusts" (Rom. 13:14, NASB). Holiness is a constant battle our entire lives.

Holiness in a person's life is like a well-tended garden. With proper attention—weeding, cultivation, planting, fertilizing, and watering, a garden thrives and produces a rich variety of useful and beautiful plants. Left to itself, however, the weeds quickly take over, and the good plants die off. It seems like the weeds are indigenous to the soil and grow on their own, while the good plants need proactive attention to create and maintain the right environment for them to grow and thrive. So too is the life of holiness. It is a proactive pursuit. If you don't *proactively* pursue holiness, then you will *reactively* suffer the consequences of sin. There's no middle ground!

And one more important aspect of holiness—men in particular have a tendency to compartmentalize their lives.

They're not always the same person at work that they are at home or church. Holiness involves transparent integrity, honestly facing the sin in our lives. Even though we perform different roles at work, home, and church, we are the same person. Certain roles have a way of exposing different aspects of our character, and all of these need sanctification. We may retain a tendency toward certain faults and weaknesses, but we can be honest about them, humbly acknowledging that numerous areas of our lives need transformation.

Jerry Bridges, in his seminal book *The Pursuit of Holiness*, compared the life of holiness to the life of farming. God is sovereign, but man is responsible. In other words, God causes the seed to germinate, and brings the rain and sun. But the farmer plows and plants, fertilizes and cultivates. In order to reap a successful harvest, the farmer is dependent on God to do what only God can do, but he also fulfills his own responsibilities. So too is the pursuit of holiness. God has empowered us by his Spirit to live a life of holiness, but has given us the responsibility to do it![73] Holiness, therefore, follows a *critical mass* of character transformation. It begins at salvation when we're first made holy in Christ, and progresses to sanctification as we become holy like Christ.

6. Relationships

*I*f *relationships* are the fabric of life, then authentic Christian relationships are composed of the finest linen — *agape*-love. Various forms of love exist in the natural world, including *eros, phileo,* and *agape,* but there exists a supernatural form of *agape*-love that comes directly from God. If you've seen this kind of *agape*, then you've seen the miraculous, because God is its only source. Those who love with this *agape* are born of God and know God, and the converse is also true. Those who do not love with this *agape* do not know God, for God is *agape*-love (1 John 4:7-8)! It's therefore important that we understand the nature of the different kinds of love since they form and fuel our relationships.

We, of course, have many types of relationships, including *family, friends,* and *community.* Even within these groups, we have family relationships with spouse, children, and other family members; friendship relationships within a local church and other ministries, and among small groups of men or women; and community relationships at work, in neighborhoods, and in other civic or service groups among outsiders and non-believers. How we treat people and relate to people is a direct result of who we are in Christ, and whether we act on the basis of who we are!

Family

Husband-Wife. The most fundamental of relationships and the essential building block of society is the marriage relationship between husband and wife. In several of his letters, Paul makes what first appears to be an unusual statement, instructing husbands to *agape*-love their wives, but wives to be subject to and respect their husbands (Eph. 5:22-25, 33; Col. 3:18-19). Why did he say it that way, and why the distinction? Let's start with the husband.

In Ephesians 5:33, Paul instructed men to love their wives as they loved themselves, which sounds very similar to the second part of the *Great Commandment* in Matthew 22:35-40. There, Jesus was asked by a lawyer to identify the greatest commandment in all the law. He said that the first and greatest commandment was to love God with your whole being—heart, soul and mind. Then he said that the second was like it, to love your neighbor as yourself. All the law and the prophets were summed up in these two commandments. Jesus had succinctly summarized the totality of the Mosaic law and prophetic writings in two statements, and thereby signified the preeminence of *agape*-love. Husbands, therefore, ought to love their wives as their own bodies (Eph. 5:28). "He who loves his own wife loves himself; for no one ever hated his own flesh, but nourishes and cherishes it, just as Christ also does the church," (Eph. 5:28b-29, NASB).

But Paul took it up another notch when he told husbands to love their wives *as* Christ loved the church and gave himself up for her to sanctify her and present her holy and blameless (Eph. 5:25-27). Jesus died for his church in the ultimate act of love, setting the highest standard of *agape*. Paul's admonition sounds like the *New Commandment* in John 13:34-35, where Jesus said:

> A new command I give you: Love one
> another. As I have loved you, so you must

love one another. By this all men will know that you are my disciples, if you love one another (NIV).

What was *new* about it? Hadn't Jesus been telling them to love people all along? The key was in his use of the phrase: *"as I have loved you."* He set the bar high by the way he loved them, even to the point of death by execution for the crimes of others. Greater love has no man than this (John 15:13)! The John 13 passage also makes clear that the singular distinctive of Christians is their *agape*-love for each other, the way they relate to each other. In other words, you recognize authentic followers of Jesus by the way they love each other with the highest form of love—*agape*!

And that brings us to the ultimate question: What is this *agape* and what distinguishes it from other kinds of love? To answer that question, we have to understand that the English term *love* has vastly different meanings, including romance or passion, affection or friendship, and honor or respect. The Greek language has distinct terms for each of these, including *eros*, *phileo*, and *agape*, but the English language translates all of them as "love." *Eros* is a term not found in the New Testament, and refers to romance and sensual passion. *Phileo* is a term of affection, emotion, and feeling, and relates to friendship and brotherly love. *Agape* is a term unique to the New Testament, and not found in secular Greek writings. It's not a term of emotion, but instead refers to judgment. John MacArthur well said that *agape* is a love of choice, referring not to emotional affection, physical attraction, or family bond.[74]

Agape refers to honor, respect, esteem, reverence, and devotion. It seeks the highest good of another. It's unconditional, unselfish, undeserved, unearned, and self-sacrificing. Since it's not a love of affection, it's not dependent on or drawn out by a quality or characteristic in its object. Since it's not an impulse from feelings, it's not dependent on natural inclinations or necessarily spent on those with whom it has an affinity. *Agape* seeks the welfare of all.[75]

Supernatural *agape* emanates from the nature of God, and is not conditioned on reciprocity. That is, its sole source is God and results from an exercise of divine will in deliberate choice without cause. It is therefore primarily an initiating act, not a responsive act. All forms of natural, human love are either reciprocal in nature or based on a premise of "give-to-get." Not so with the *agape*-love of God! His love is nature-based, not object-based. He doesn't love us because of our attractive qualities or because we earn his respect. He loves us because it is his essential nature to extend love to people regardless of their position as friend or enemy. He seeks our highest good without regard to who or what we are.

In fact, while we were his enemies, God accomplished our reconciliation (Rom. 5:10). While we were helpless, Christ died for us (Rom. 5:6). God's love is "give-to-have" not "give-to-get." He extends his love to us so we can have it and know him. Men, on the other hand, love conditionally by nature or show love to get love. Even the human form of *agape* shows respect and honor only to those who have earned it. By nature, we never show *agape* to an enemy. And that's why Jesus in the Sermon on the Mount (Matt. 5-7) and the Sermon on the Plain (Luke 6) exhorted his followers to love their enemies, do good to those who hate them, bless those who curse them, and pray for those who abuse them. "If you love those who love you, what credit is that to you? For even sinners love those who love them" (Luke 6:32, NASB). Rather, he said, the supernatural mark of a son of the Most High is the honor, respect, and esteem—the *agape* he shows to all people without condition.

Husbands love your wives like that, like Jesus loves! Seek her highest good, even at your greatest cost. Lay down your life for her. Love her unconditionally, and yes, love her with great passion and affection too! For the basis for all human relationships starts with the husband loving his wife, as Scripture records with Adam and Eve. If the husband fails to love his wife, then the family ultimately fails. And if the family fails, then society fails. But God initiates the process by pouring out his *agape*-love on us by the Spirit given for this purpose (Rom. 5:5). Recall Clint Black's message in his song *Something That We Do*. The love between husband and wife isn't something that we find, or something that we're in, or someplace that we fall. It's something that we do![76]

But Paul didn't tell wives to love their husbands. Maybe they're better at it than men, and don't need help in showing love. Instead, their instructions were to submit and show respect (Eph. 5:22, 33; Col. 3:18). All of us have a hard time submitting to authority on some level, and all of us are subject to authority somewhere up the chain of command. But if I have submitted my life to the sovereignty of God, then I should have no trouble submitting to the authorities he places in my life. And that goes for all men and women. Yet God designed the husband to be the priest and leader of his family, and that's true whether we (husband *or* wife) accept it or not. "For the husband is the head of the wife as Christ is the head of the church. . . Now as the church submits to Christ, so also wives should submit to their husbands in everything" (Eph. 5:23-24, NIV). Genesis 2:18 shows that women were subordinate to men in the order of creation.

Even within the Trinity there exists a hierarchy of authority. The Son submits to the Father (John 5:19, 30), while the Holy Spirit spotlights the Son (John 15:26). Likewise, the church submits to Christ (Eph. 5:24), church members submit to their leaders (Heb. 13:17), and people submit to governing authorities, because all "authorities that exist have been established by God" (Rom. 13:1, NIV). But subordination should not be confused with inferiority. Wives are not inferior to their husbands, who were challenged by the Apostle Peter to honor their wives as *fellow heirs* of the grace of life (1Peter 3:7). Wives, in turn, honor God by respectfully submitting to their husbands as to the Lord (Eph. 5:22; 1 Peter 3:1-2).

Parent-Child. After the husband-wife relationship, clearly the most important family relationship is between parent and child. I only scratched the surface on the husband-wife relationship, and I'll do even less on the parent-child relationship. Volumes have been written by experts on both topics, and especially the latter by notable Christian counselors, so I won't attempt to do the same. But I have been married to Janet, my lovely wife, for over 30 years (and counting!) and have raised three wonderful children to adulthood, Stuart, Daniel, and Susannah. So I have some experience in the trenches of parenthood.

Perhaps the most challenging aspect of relating to children is that they're always changing on you. Just when you get used them, they grow up a little more, and that changes the dynamics of the relationship. It gets more complicated when they hit the teenage and young adult years, and you move away from controlling everything in their lives to giving them more freedom to make their own decisions. But with freedom comes responsibility, and with responsibility comes accountability. And that makes for stress in relationships.

What do our kids most need from us? *Love* and *discipline*. As a parent, you want to be fair, firm, and fun. You want to strive to relate to them, show them genuine love, and connect with them at every age. At the same time, since you are the primary authority in their lives, you must fairly administer discipline as you build into them a strong sense of respect and responsibility. And you want to have a lot of fun with them, make a lot of good memories, and enjoy them for the short time you have them!

I've already discussed aspects of biblical love, which also relate to parent-child relationships. With discipline, however, our culture has changed the way we regard it. When I was young, the watchword of traditional fathers was that "kids are to be seen and not heard." Today, we've swung to the other extreme, and "Disney" dads will do most anything to make their kids like them. So let me address my comments on discipline primarily to fathers. We need to find the balance between Proverbs 23:13 and Ephesians 5:4:

> Do not withhold discipline from a child; if you punish him with the rod, he will not die (Prov. 23:13, NIV).

> Fathers, do not exasperate your children; instead, bring them up in the training and instruction of the Lord (Eph.5:4, NIV).

We want our children to know that we *love* and *care* for them, but we must teach them *respect* and *responsibility*. My parents, Paul and Carolyn Sanders, were particularly good at teaching me respect for those in authority and personal responsibility for my actions. If we don't, then our children pay a high price later when they can't function as mature adults. The parent-child relationship necessarily involves training and instruction, but we need to patiently discipline where needed, and avoid exasperating our children by unloading our anger and frustration when they fail. If we expect to maintain healthy relationships with our children, we must strive to faithfully address issues of character and behavior without condemning them as imperfect or inadequate. I remember a similar distinction that the Holy Spirit convicts a person of specific acts and attitudes of sin, while Satan condemns a person generally and in total.

Many parents aren't that good at disciplining their children. In anger they lash out and demoralize their kids. Instead, we should patiently discipline our children as those we love, just as the Lord does us (Heb. 12:6). Afterwards, it yields the peaceable fruit of righteousness (Heb. 12:11), and your children will respect you, if not now, then later. They also need to be held accountable for their actions. Even if now they don't fully appreciate it, they will bless you when they're grown! And I say that from personal experience.

In relating to my children through the years, I've tried to take an interest in the things they were interested in. It allowed us to spend more time together and afforded many opportunities for life lessons. When my sons were young, they played little league baseball, and my oldest son Stuart became a baseball fanatic, pitching through high school. So I spent many years catching for him, throwing batting practice, and hitting grounders and fly balls. They also played football through high school, so we played a lot of punt, pass and kick! I was only moderately good at these sports, but the time we spent together was invaluable.

My younger son, Daniel, is the doctor in the family, winning the science fair as a high school freshman. That year, he designed and built a medieval trebuchet, similar to a catapult, and I filmed him launching a basketball across the backyard and swishing it in the basketball goal! We also played golf together when he took it up in high school. With my daughter, Susannah, it was more challenging. She and Janet have a great relationship and did many mother-daughter things together, but I had to work harder to find ways to connect with her in her world and expose her to mine. She came and worked as a clerk in my law office several summers, and that gave us many opportunities for discussions about life and work.

In the end, the most important thing is to *talk* to your kids. Make a regular habit of talking to your children, discussing and explaining things as they come up, maintaining an ongoing dialogue about everything in life, especially spiritual things. I don't mean lecturing your kids, but talking to them, instructing them, and helping them process. When they're young, they won't entirely get it, but my kids have told me that they remember what was discussed and it makes sense now that they're grown. When they're teenagers, their openness comes and goes, but stick with them even when they seem closed. They need both sound counsel and understanding even more.

Stay informed about who their friends are, what they're interested in, who they admire, and what they value. Parents can and should be the most influential people in their lives, but only if they stick with them through good times and bad. Kids may pull away for a season in high school or college, but they'll come back if you keep reaching out to them and be there for them. Your kids are not your buddies, but they are your closest relatives after your spouse. Mentor your kids! Disciple your kids! Read and study the Bible with them. Have family devotions with them. Pray with them. Model the faith for them. Teach them to read the word and pray regularly. Make lasting investments in their lives, and seek their highest good. You get to mold and shape them, and you get to help them grow to become the mature, fruitful adults that God wants them to be.

And since you're the most influential people in determining who they become, take the initiative to speak into their lives, and in a healthy way address areas of sin and selfishness that retard their progress to maturity. Don't worry about whether they like you or not. They probably won't at times. But seek their greater good and faithfully parent them through the mine fields of youth. Along the way, don't forget to enjoy your children. You only have them for a season and its much shorter than you realize, though it seems to go on forever! It doesn't. Have fun with them, go on vacations with them, and create experiences they'll remember for a lifetime!

But don't live your life through your children. And don't make them live up to your expectations of performing well at *your* favorite sport or discipline. They're not your hobby or past time. And it's not their purpose to fulfill your unmet dreams. Help them find what they're gifted at and interested in, and help them excel there! They're unique, so treat them that way. Help them discover how God has fashioned them, and help them become everything he wants them to be. This certainly includes the well-rounded and mature development in all essential areas of life, but inspire and lead them! Don't guilt them into expected levels of behavior and performance. Parents have the opportunity to make the greatest impact on their children, and don't want to be the source of their greatest hang-ups.

Friends

Our society has become increasingly isolated, and people have fewer and fewer trusted friends. People are flat lonely, and they think they like it that way, but they don't and it's unhealthy. We need close friendships, and I don't mean acquaintances. We have many of those—too many! But we don't have many close friends. That's especially true for men. Women generally do better than men at real friendships. It's not uncommon for the women's groups and Bible studies in churches to thrive, while the men's groups pale in comparison. Men are busy, and men are loners. So I'll address my comments mainly to men.

We think we're supposed to be like John Wayne, the quintessential American—fiercely independent, in need of no one, a lone ranger riding off into the sunset. But at the risk of sounding sac-religious, I'd like to state categorically: it ain't so! The biblical model is shown in the relationship between Jonathan and David in 1 Samuel 18-20 and 2 Samuel 1. These two men were fierce warriors in their own right. One was the courageous son of a king and heir-apparent to the throne. The other was the greatest of all Israelite kings.

Jonathan single-handedly led the charge against the Philistines when the two opposing armies were stuck in gridlock on opposite hills at the pass at Michmash (1 Samuel 14:1-23). He led an uphill charge with his armor bearer, stating that nothing prevented the Lord from saving by many or by few! His faith and bravery mobilized the entire Israelite army, including the cowards and turncoats, to achieve a great victory in Israel. You might recall that David had a similar experience during an international tension involving Goliath! He couldn't understand why the Israelites stood passively on one mountain while the Philistines taunted them from the other. He volunteered to face the giant in a winner-take-all contest between the two nations, knowing that the battle belonged to the Lord (1 Samuel 17)! It did. He won, and David became a hero and the next king.

These two great heroes were tough, manly men, but they shared a close, loyal friendship that was thicker even than blood. And on the issue of toughness, let me point out as an aside that John Wayne won his many battles from the old West through Vietnam using guns and rifles. David and Jonathan, however, won their battles with swords and an occasional sling shot! Who was tougher? And yet Scripture records that "the soul of Jonathan was knit to the soul of David, and Jonathan loved him as himself" (1 Samuel 18:1, NASB). These men stuck together through thick and thin even when Jonathan had to stand up to his corrupt father who was trying to kill David to ensure that Jonathan ascended the throne. Jonathan would have none of it and supported his friend to the end. They made a covenant with each other to stay loyal friends (1 Samuel 18:3, 20:8).

When the strain from King Saul became too great, David was forced to flee. The last time that David and Jonathan saw each other, "they kissed each other and wept together" (1 Samuel 20:42, NASB). These grown men and warriors cried and blubbered over each other when they parted for the last time! Jonathan always had David's back and helped him safely escape. When later Jonathan was killed in the battle that ended Saul's reign, David sang a lament for his closest friend:

> Your beauty, O Israel, is slain on your high places!
> How the mighty have fallen!. . .
> How the mighty have fallen in the midst of the battle!
> Jonathan is slain on your high places.
> I am distressed for you, my brother Jonathan;
> You have been very pleasant to me.
> Your love to me was more wonderful

Than the love of women.
(2 Samuel 1:17-19, 25-26, NASB.)

Did you get that? The love of his friend and fellow warrior, the guy who had his back, was better than the love of women. What does that mean? He's not talking about emotion or sensuality. He's referring to the highest form of *agape*-love, using the Hebrew equivalent—the love that sacrificially seeks the highest good of another—to describe the quality of their friendship! Do you have a friend like that, a guy you can rely on no matter what? You should! The enemy picks off lone rangers.

David's son, King Solomon, understood the value and strength of trusted friends:

> Two are better than one because they have a good return for their labor. For if either of them falls, the one will lift up his companion. But woe to the one who falls when there is not another to lift him up. . . . And if one can overpower him who is alone, two can resist him. A cord of three strands is not quickly torn apart. (Eccl. 4:9-10, 12, NASB.)

Gary Desalvo of Temple Bible Church talks about the "Hole in the Roof Gang" from Luke 5:17-20.[77] Jesus was teaching in a crowded house when a group of men tried to bring their paralyzed friend to him to be healed. When they couldn't get him in the door, they hauled him up on the roof and let him down through the tiles. Now those are the kind of friends you want—guys who have your back and help you carry the load when it's too heavy. We need friends who will support us no matter what, but who will also get in our face when we need it. We need both the *encouragement* and *accountability* of close, trusted friends, both the positive and the negative.

And we need to play both sides of the ball, offense and defense. We need brothers who go into battle with us both in life and ministry (offense), and brothers who carry us to the MASH tent to heal up when we're wounded (defense). I've had the privilege of sharing such a friendship with long-time friend, Dean Murray. In fact, I could write a treatise of all the things we've been through, both highs and lows, since we met our freshman year in college. It's been quite a journey from college to middle age, and the best is yet to come!

Community

As clichéd as it sounds, we do well to remember that the local church is not a building or a hub of information, but rather a fellowship of believers living in *community*. Church is not simply a place where we gather to attend a meeting, sitting in rows, staring at the backs of other heads, and listening to one guy talk. The church is an interactive organism, composed of many different parts, all of them vital to the well-being of the entire body. Yet in the "information age," we're often isolated in our own churches. We're inundated with information, but starved for real human interaction and fellowship.

How can that possibly be when the local church has every modern convenience? Get with the program! Maybe that's the problem — *the program*. The church has too many meetings to attend, too many programs to run, too much bureaucracy to maintain. I've got to find a place to hide from the avalanche of *local church* before it buries me! How did we get here? Superior organization and management! But instead of promoting community, it can hinder it. Real community is more organic than it is organizational, just like disciplemaking. Organization can support and stimulate, but not replace, organic community. In the end, it's about relationships, and relationships don't happen on a schedule. Meetings and programs happen on a schedule. Relationships take time and effort.

My wife Janet taught me this very important lesson years ago. I live by my schedule, and there are three things I don't tolerate well—crowds, lines, and traffic. So when the church service ended, I was usually the first one out the door to beat the crowd and avoid the traffic. Fellowship was expendable! She asked how we would get to know anyone if we run out the door every Sunday. Janet is much more relational than I am, and a better listener and conversationalist. She's also very patient with slow learners like me. I finally learned to slow down, set aside my schedule, and take time to get to know people. I found that when I asked questions, learned their backgrounds and interests, that most people are much more interesting than they first let on! I might even learn something and benefit from their friendship!

Men are often blind to their need for fellowship because they have a tendency to isolate themselves (the John Wayne effect). But in doing so, they become self-absorbed and reject sound judgment (Prov. 18:1). We need to spend time with others in order to motivate and encourage ourselves toward love and good works (Heb. 10:24-25). The Christian life is a team sport! Lone rangers lose. Rocks in a rock tumbler don't get smooth because they bounce off the walls of the tumbler. They get smooth because they bounce off the other rocks! We need fellowship to smooth off the rough edges, and help maintain a proper sense of balance and perspective. We also learn from each other.

We have a tendency to congregate around people we like and who are like us. But fellowship in a local church forces us to relate to people we might not otherwise be around, and that edifies the whole body. As Paul said in 1 Corinthians 12:

> The body is a unit, though it is made up
> of many parts; and though all its parts are

many, they form one body. . . . But in fact God
has arranged the parts of the body, every one
of them, just as he wanted them to be. If they
were all one part, where would the body be?
As it is, there are many parts, but one body.
The eye cannot say to the hand, "I don't need
you!" And the head cannot say to the feet,
"I don't need you!" On the contrary, those
parts of the body that seem to be weaker are
indispensable, and the parts we think are
less honorable we treat with special honor. (1
Cor. 12:12, 18-23a, NIV.)

God intends that there be no division in the body. If one
part suffers, every part suffers, and if one part is honored,
every part rejoices. Each of us is part of the body of Christ
(1 Cor. 12:25-27).

Janet and I experienced this first hand after she had surgery to correct a congenital heart defect in 1999. Both of us
had served for many years at our church in College Station.
She has the serving gifts, and I have the speaking gifts (1
Peter 4:10-11). Just prior to her surgery, we were considering
a move to Virginia where I'd received two job offers. While
considering the move, we had a "George Bailey" crisis
thinking that no one would miss us or much care if we left,
despite our many friends and years of service. Our community shocked us, however, with a generous outpouring
of support and comfort during her surgery. Janet received
so many flowers at the hospital that the staff thought she
must be a celebrity when we wheeled out the loaded carts at
check-out. At home, we received fresh, hot food every day
for six solid weeks! We had to invite the neighbors over to
help us eat it all. I must say, we were overwhelmed by the
outpouring of love from our community. It was an incredible show of gratitude for Janet's testimony, friendship, and
faithful service.

Relationships spring from a heart of *agape*-love — a self-sacrificing love devoted to the glory of God and the welfare of men, a love that both empowers and compels us to love other people. But what about those who are not part of our community? How do we relate to outsiders and non-believers in the workplace, in our neighborhoods, and in our civic or service groups? Chapter 8 addresses these and other ministry issues.

7. Doctrine

*I*t may seem dry or even divisive to consider *doctrine* in this book, but a committed disciple of Jesus will embrace the centrality of the word of God to the whole of life. "For the word of God is living and active and sharper than any two-edged sword, and piercing as far as the division of soul and spirit, of both joints and marrow, and able to judge the thoughts and intentions of the heart" (Heb. 4:12, NASB). There's never been a time when there existed so many different English translations of the Bible. Prior to World War II, the only major English translation was the King James Version, although it had been awhile since we spoke in its vernacular! And yet, I wonder if there's ever been a time when general biblical literacy has been lower. At one time, Bible truths were foundational to our basic worldview, but not anymore. Even for those who know the Bible, many take a *low view* of its truthfulness or relevance. For the Christian, however, a proficient knowledge of Bible teachings is of critical importance. Therefore, I wish to advocate and reinforce a *high view* of Scripture.

Many volumes have been written on the broad subject of Christian doctrine. I can't begin to address even the highlights. So let me address *three seminal issues*, the authority of Scripture in the lives of believers, the nature and distinctions of law and grace, and a brief summary of precepts essential to the faith. Paul exhorted the church elders in every town to hold firmly to the trustworthy message (or faithful word) as it had been taught, so that they could encourage others by *sound doctrine* and refute those who oppose it (Titus 1:9). The truths of Scripture are under full-scale assault on a multitude of fronts. The enemy well knows that if the foundation cracks, the whole building crumbles! But Jesus said that his words would *never* pass away, though heaven and earth will (Matt. 24:35; Mark 13:31). Such is the reliability and permanence of the word of God! Thus, everyone who hears the word and lives by it, has built his life on the solid, immoveable rock, which is impervious to wind, rain, and flood (Matt. 7:24-25).

Authority of Scripture

A central tenet of the Protestant Reformation was *sola scriptura*, the doctrine that Scripture alone is authoritative for the faith and practice of Christians. For centuries, the church had elevated the traditions and opinions of men, especially papal authority, to a status equal with Scripture. Yet the Bible alone is the highest authority for the Christian faith, and believers reject any tradition or teaching that is not in full agreement with it. The authority of Scripture is supreme and universal *because* it is God's word.

Dr. Norman Geisler points out:

The Bible claims to be a book from God, a message with divine authority. Indeed, the biblical writers say they were moved by the Holy Spirit to utter His very words — that their message came by revelation so that what they wrote was breathed out (inspired) by God Himself.

. . .

The extent of divine authority in Scripture includes:

(1) all that is written — 2 Tim. 3:16;
(2) even the very words — Matt. 22:43;
1 Cor.2:13;
(3) and tenses of verbs — Matt. 22:32;
Gal. 3:16;
(4) even the smallest parts of the words —
Matt. 5:17-18.

That is, even though the Bible was not mechanically dictated by God to man, nonetheless, the result is just as perfect as if it had been. The biblical authors claimed that God is the source of the very words of Scripture, since He supernaturally superintended the process by which they wrote, using their own vocabulary and style to record His message (2 Peter 1:20-21).[78]

Liberals, on the other hand, believe that *authority* resides in the reasoning of man, not the revelation of God through the Bible. This fallacy contradicts the Bible's divine authority, as Dr. Ryrie pointed out:

To the liberal, the Bible is entirely the product of human reasoning and thus contains only man's thoughts about God and the world and himself. It is the history of man's development of his religious beliefs, but it is not a message from a transcendent God who breaks into history from the outside.[79]

The main New Testament passage on the *authority* of the Bible is found 2 Timothy 3:16-17, which states:

All Scripture is inspired by God and profitable for teaching, for reproof, for correction, for training in righteousness; so that the man of God may be adequate (complete), equipped for every good work (NASB).

The NIV translation says that all Scripture is *God-breathed* and *useful*. Thus, Paul said that every Scripture is inspired and every Scripture is useful! Peter also said that Scripture's "prophecy never had its origin in the will of man, but men spoke from God as they were carried along by the Holy Spirit" (2 Peter 1:21, NIV).

The Greek term translated "God-breathed," "breathed out by God," or "inspired by God" is *theopneustos*, and does not occur in any other Greek text, biblical or otherwise, prior to the letter of Second Timothy. Paul may have coined this term himself from words meaning "God" and "breathed." And Paul does not point to the human authors as inspired people, but says that the writings themselves, the very words, are spoken or breathed out by God.[80] "God's words were given through men superintended by the Holy Spirit so that their writings are without error."[81]

Dr. Geisler defines *inspiration* as follows:

Inspiration is the supernatural operation of the Holy Spirit, who through the different personalities and literary styles of the chosen human authors invested the very words of the original books of Holy Scripture, alone and in their entirety, as the very Word of God without error in all that they teach or imply (including history and science), and the Bible is thereby the infallible rule and final authority for faith and practice of all believers.[82]

It's important to note that biblical inspiration is both *verbal* and *plenary*. It's verbal in that the words themselves are inspired, not just the idea or the writer. It's plenary meaning that it extends to every part of the words and all they teach or imply.[83]

The Bible is *inspired* and therefore *useful* for directing the course of our lives, for reproving us when we get off track, for making course corrections, and for training us in Christlike righteousness. But the Bible's usefulness is only realized if properly interpreted, understood, and applied. And that leads us to a brief discussion on *hermeneutics* and *inductive Bible study methods*. (Don't worry, it won't be long or dry!)

Hermeneutics is a theological term for the study or science of interpreting Scripture, and includes the principles and methodology of *exegesis*. The term *exegesis* means to draw the meaning out of a text. Contrast that with *eisegesis*, which means to read your own interpretation into a text. Exegesis presumes to interpret the text objectively, while eisegesis involves subjective interpretation.[84] Exegesis involves the exposition, explanation, and critical interpretation of a text. In essence, exegesis is applied hermeneutics, which seeks to interpret what an author has written. More specifically:

> Biblical exegesis is a systematic process by which a person arrives at a reasonable and coherent sense of the meaning and message of a biblical passage. . . . In the process of exegesis, a passage must be viewed in its historical and grammatical context with its time/purpose of writing taken into account. This is often accommodated by asking:
>
> - Who wrote the text, and who is the intended readership?
> - What is the context of the text, i.e. how does it fit in the author's larger thought process, purpose, or argument in the chapter and book where it resides?

- Is the choice of words, wording, or word order significant in this particular passage?
- Why was the text written (e.g. to correct, encourage, or explain, etc.)?
- When was the text written?[85]

Similar hermeneutic questions include:

- What is the cultural, historical context?
- What was the author's original intended meaning?
- How did the author's contemporaries understand him?
- Why did he say it that way?[86]

The goal of hermeneutics is "to accurately handle the word of truth" (2 Tim. 2:15, NASB), in striving to accurately discern the meaning of a text.[87] The Golden Rule of hermeneutics according to Martin Luther was that "if the *plain sense* makes *good sense*, seek no other sense."[88] In other words, give the text its normal, natural meaning, seeking the obvious, customary meaning of words and phrases used. Give a passage its plain, literal meaning unless the context is clearly otherwise (i.e. metaphor or figure of speech). I was taught in law school that every contract provision must be interpreted in the context in which it was written. As my pastor, Grant Kaul, said, the focus of Scripture interpretation is not on what the passage means *to you*, but on what the passage *means* as intended by the author. And let Scripture interpret Scripture, because the best commentary on the Bible is the Bible itself. [89]

One of the most effective ways to interpret Scripture is through *inductive* Bible study, which involves drawing out of truth from a biblical text. It includes at least three key components, including *observation, interpretation,* and *appli-*

cation, and some would add a fourth, *correlation*, that may be simply described as follows:

> *Observation* — What does it say?
> *Interpretation* — What does it mean?
> *Correlation* — How do cross references use similar words
>   or phrases?
> *Application* — How can you apply it in your life?

This straight-forward method for studying the Bible stimulates the student to dig deeper and mine the rich deposit of the word. "I rejoice at Your word as one who finds great treasure" (Psalm 119:162, NKJV). Utilizing this four-part inductive study format, we can seek to understand and then apply the word! "But prove yourselves doers of the word, and not merely hearers who delude themselves" (James 1:22, NASB). Understanding is valueless if you don't live it out.

Law & Grace

In Chapter 4, I discussed the general nature of grace, contrasting it with the concepts of merit and judgment. Here, I'd like to focus on the interrelationship and distinctions between *law* and *grace*. Fundamental to our belief systems are the doctrines of law and grace. By nature, we impose the burdens of law on others, especially as their actions affect us, but we're quick to excuse ourselves when the shoe's on the other foot. Our innate egocentricity is to blame. As for grace, we often believe that it's simply too good to be *completely* true, or we just take it for granted. Perhaps our cynicism and apathy are to blame. But let's take a look at law and grace from God's point of view, since he's the one who created them.

As a lawyer, I'm trained to qualify my statements to avoid absolutes and keep from being impeached with the inevitable exception. But let me make an utterly dogmatic statement—from God's perspective, there are only *two kinds* of people in the world, those who live *under law* and those who live *under grace*. There are no other options, and if you're not under grace, then by default you're under law, whether you know it or not.

The original purposes of God's law were to: (1) reveal his standard of holiness, (2) prescribe worship practices, (3) direct human conduct, (4) govern society, (5) identify sin in all its manifestations, (6) provide a temporary remedy for unintentional sins, and (7) impose just consequences for violators. The law by its nature is good, bringing order out of chaos, fairness out of prejudice, and integrity out of injustice. Those who know and love the law of God are wise beyond their years:

> O how I love Your law! It is my meditation all the day. Your commandments make me wiser than my enemies, for they are ever mine. I have more insight than all my teachers, for your testimonies are my meditation. I understand more than the aged, because I have observed Your precepts (Psalm 119:97-100, NASB).

The law, therefore, sets the perfect standard. In fact, it sets a standard so perfect, to the fullest measure of God's righteousness, that no mere mortal can attain it. The law was designed to set the absolute standard of righteous living, but it does not empower a person to live up to that standard, nor was it meant to. The law was meant to set the bar, not enable a person to meet it. In fact, it exposes our inadequacies, not our competencies. As a result, we're prone to think the law itself defective because it prescribes without empowering, but that belies its underlying purpose—to point out our fallen state. As Dr. Barclay noted:

> The trouble with the law has always been that it can diagnose the malady but cannot effect a cure. Law shows a man where he goes wrong, but does not help him avoid going wrong. There is in fact. . . a kind of terrible paradox in law. It is human nature that when a fruit is forbidden it has a tendency to become desirable. "Stolen fruits are sweetest." Law, therefore, can actually move a man to desire the very thing which it forbids.[90]

Despite this paradox, men seek to justify themselves by observing the law, or more likely, their preferred version of it. Men will submit to a law of their choosing if it leads to the acceptance and success they seek. Years ago, I assisted another attorney on a complex car-fire case. The opposing attorney was very successful and worked for a large, national law firm, but would soon be forced out by the firm's strict retirement policy. My friend was sympathetic, but commented gravely that the other guy "lived under a lot of rules."

Those who live under the law also seek to earn God's favor through performance and rule-keeping, and strive to measure up to his expectations by their own efforts. They fail of course, but you can't convince them otherwise. It's all they know, and they can't conceive of a universe that doesn't require them to *do something* to achieve results. Deluded by pride, they believe they're good enough, being completely unmindful of reality. The law serves to inflame the sinful nature in every man. And even when he desires to do what is good, he can't carry it out. Thus, the law actually condemns the one who tries to keep it. (*See* Rom. 7:18-24.)

In God's eyes, all of man's righteous acts are nothing more than filthy rags (Isaiah 64:6). Citing multiple Old Testament passages, Paul summarized God's indictments of those under the law in Romans 3:10-18, (NIV):

As it is written:
"There is no one righteous, not even one;
there is no one who understands, no one
seeks God. All have turned away, they have
together become worthless; there is no one
who does good, not even one."
"Their throats are open graves; their tongues
practice deceit."
"The poison of vipers is on their lips."
"Their mouths are full of cursing and bit-
terness."
"Their feet are swift to shed blood; ruin and
misery mark their ways, and the way of
peace they do not know."
"There is no fear of God before their eyes."

Paul then concluded, "Therefore, no one will be declared
righteous in his sight by *observing the law*; rather, through the
law we become conscious of sin" (Rom. 4:20, NIV, emphasis
added). In his famous 1741 sermon, *Sinners in the Hands of
an Angry God*, Jonathan Edwards stated:

Your wickedness makes you as it were heavy
as lead, and to tend downwards with great
weight and pressure towards Hell; and if
God should let you go, you would immediately sink and swiftly descend & plunge into
the bottomless gulf, and your healthy constitution, and your own care and prudence, and
best contrivance, and all your righteousness,
would have no more influence to uphold
you and keep you out of hell, than a spider's
web would have to stop a falling rock.

Those who live under grace, on the other hand, have
been justified before God as a result of the perfect sacrifice of
God's own son, Jesus. Under the law, every man is respon-

sible for his own actions and subject to judgment. Under grace, people of faith are excused from the permanent consequences of their actions and their sinful nature, because one man—one God-man perfectly kept the law, and himself suffered the condemnation of everyone else that broke it. God allows Jesus' sacrifice to be imputed to us. To be justified is to be acquitted or declared righteous. "It is a legal term used of a favorable verdict in a trial. The word depicts a courtroom setting, with God presiding as the Judge, determining the faithfulness of each person to the law."[91]

> Therefore, there is now no condemnation for those who are in Christ Jesus, because through Christ Jesus the law of the Spirit of life set me free from the law of sin and death. For what the law was powerless to do in that it was weakened by the sinful nature, God did by sending his own Son in the likeness of sinful man to be a sin offering. And so he condemned sin in sinful man, in order that the righteous requirements of the law might be fully met in us, who do not live according to the sinful nature but according to the Spirit (Rom. 8:1-4, NIV).

The law was given to expose sin, and grace was given to excuse it. "Christ redeemed us from the curse of the law by becoming a curse for us" (Gal. 3:13, NIV). By the grace of God—the unmerited and unearned favor of God, through faith in Jesus, we've been empowered by God's Spirit to live a worthwhile and eternal life! Life under the law is lived by rules. Life under grace is lived through relationship. The rules bring death. The relationship brings life! The law was our tutor to lead us to Christ, and by grace we are justified through faith in Christ (Gal. 3:24). Grace enables, grace empowers, and grace uplifts!

Essential Theology

Theology is the study of God, or a rational discourse about God, including essential Christian beliefs.[92] More than any other topic I'll discuss, this one has generated mass volumes of writings. So it seems presumptuous of me to address what I've called "essential theology." I'm aware that only a lawyer can write a forty page document and call it a "brief." But I'm also mindful of the old adage, "I would have written you a shorter memo if I'd had more time." Thus, I will attempt to summarize key concepts on a few major areas of theology. Earlier in this chapter, I discussed *the inspiration of Scripture, law,* and *grace.* In Chapter 4, I touched on topics of *sin, judgment, salvation, faith, heaven,* and *hell.* In Chapter 6, I addressed *church community.*

These are among the more important issues of faith in areas of what is commonly called *systematic theology.* Over the last two centuries, various branches of the church have compromised or "punted" on these and other essential doctrines.

I'm not attempting to write a theological tome, but let me briefly address five additional topics: *God and the Trinity, the Deity of Christ, the work of the Holy Spirit, the importance of creation,* and *lessons from biblical and church history.* I've obviously left out a number of important topics and sub-topics, choosing to focus on a few key topics, acknowledging that I'm only touching on the issues. Far more qualified men have written exhaustive treatises on all subjects of systematic theology.

God and the Trinity. God is the only constant. Everything else and all other doctrines revolve around him. God created and gave existence to everything there is in heaven and earth. The attributes or characteristics of God include, among many others, his holiness, righteousness, omnipotence, omniscience, omnipresence, love, and wisdom. He is infinite, glorious, perfect, eternal, just, merciful, and sovereign. And God is the Heavenly Father! He is the father of

Israel (Ex. 4:22); he is the father of Jesus (Matt. 3:17); he is the father of all believers in Christ (Gal. 3:26); and he is the father of all (Acts 17:29).[93]

There is only one God (monotheism), but there are three distinct persons in that one God (the Trinity): the Father, the Son, and the Holy Spirit (Matt. 28:19). The concept of the Trinity does not mean that there are three gods (tritheism) or that God has three modes of one and the same being (modalism). God is triune, referring both to his "threeness" and unity. "He is plurality within unity. God has a plurality of persons and a unity of essence; God is three persons in one nature." Therefore, Jesus Christ and the Holy Spirit are not inferior to God the Father (unitarianism). The three members of the Trinity are equal in essence, but have different roles. As Dr. Geisler summarized, "the Father is the Planner, the Son is the Accomplisher, and the Holy Spirit is the Applier of salvation to believers. The Father is the Source, the Son is the Means, and the Holy Spirit is the Effector of salvation. . ."[94]

The Deity of Christ. Essential to the concept of the Trinity is the deity of Christ. The Apostle John records that Jesus was in the beginning with God and all things were made through him (John 1:1-3, 14). Jesus is the living word of God, the physical manifestation of God in human form (John 1:1, 14; Col. 1:15; 2 Cor. 4:4). Throughout history, many have denied the deity of Christ, including today's liberals and Unitarians. But to do so is to undermine the central tenets of Christianity by removing the divine savior, his virgin birth, miracles, and resurrection. Jesus is not just a good man, great teacher, or some sort of wise philosopher. He didn't leave us that option. It's really all or none! He's either everything he said he was, or he's an outright fraud or nutcase. As C. S. Lewis famously said in his trilemma to prove the divinity of Jesus, he's either Lord, liar, or lunatic.[95]

Jesus himself claimed equality with God (John 5:18, 8:58, 14:9-10). God the Father attested to Jesus' divinity (Matt. 3:17; John 5:22-23, 37-38). Both the Old Testament prophets and New Testament apostles attested to his divinity (Isaiah 9:6; Micah 5:2; Zech. 12:10; John 1:1, 14; Phil. 2:6; Col. 1:15-17). He was actually resurrected from the dead, and without this singular event, there is no Christianity (Luke 24:6-7; John 20: 9, 15-16; Acts 2:31-32; 1 Cor. 15:16-19). After his resurrection, Jesus ascended into heaven to sit at the right hand of God, and reigns as the King of Kings and Lord of Lords (Luke 22:69, 24:51; John 20:17; Acts 1:9, 7:55; Rev. 17:14, 19:16)!

The Work of the Holy Spirit. Perhaps the least under-stood member of the Trinity, the Holy Spirit is the divine person present and active on the earth today. His role among us on behalf of the kingdom of God is indispensable. And let's be clear that the Holy Spirit is a person, not merely a force or a thing. He has a mind (Rom. 8:27), emotions (Eph. 4:30), and will (1 Cor. 12:11). He was present at Jesus' baptism, and he empowered Jesus' ministry (Luke 3:22, 4:1, 14, 18). After his resurrection, Jesus sent him to us to serve as our helper, counselor, and advocate (John 14:16-17, 26, 15:26, 16:7). The Greek word *paraclete*, from which these terms derive, refers to one who comes alongside another, and pleads the cause of another.[96]

His work in the lives of believers is all-encompassing. He convicts the world of sin, righteousness, and judgment (John 16:8-11). He regenerates and causes the new birth (John 3:5-8; Titus 3:5). He baptizes, indwells, seals, fills, and empowers believers (1 Cor. 12:13, 6:19; Eph. 1:13, 4:30, 5:18; Rom. 15:13, 19). He gives spiritual gifts to all members of the body (1 Cor. 12:4-11). He leads, guides, and teaches the followers of Jesus (John 16:12-15; Acts 13:4; Gal. 5:18; Rom. 8:14; 1 Cor. 2:13). And he builds character in the form of fruits of the Spirit (Gal. 5:22-23)![97]

The Importance of Creation. " 'In the beginning God created the heavens and the earth' (Gen. 1:1). With these majestic words, the Scriptures begin their description of the origin of all things, and creation is the foundation for every-thing else that follows."[98] The battle over *origins* is among the most heated, for if God can be eliminated at the beginning, then the atheistic-evolutionary worldview prevails. Prior to modern evolution, every intellectual non-Christian had to admit at least that there was some sort of supernatural intelligence that started it all. But not now. The intellectual elites have dismissed God altogether, because matter, in their view, has always existed. And given a little time and chance, anything can evolve. Hence, our present array of life forms. Really?

Here's the question they can't answer: where did the first *living* cell come from? In other words, what was the original cause from which all life evolved? No clue! In reality, modern evolution is the product of the rebellious and unbelieving heart of man who wants no accountability to a sovereign God. All life exists because God created it! God is the *origin*. And following Genesis, Scripture is replete with references to the creation story as an historical fact (Ex. 20:11; Psalm 8:3-6; Matt. 19:4-5; Mark 10:6-7; Rom. 1:20, 5:12-14; 1 Cor. 11:9, 15:22, 45; 2 Cor. 11:3; 1 Tim. 2:13-14; Jude 14).[99]

Lessons from Biblical and Church History. This is not a topic of theology *per se*, but I include it here because of its impact on our theology. As they say, those who don't know their history are doomed to repeat it. "That which has been is that which will be, and that which has been done is that which will be done. So there is nothing new under the sun" (Eccl. 1:9, NASB). Inscribed on the National Archives Building in Washington D. C. is the inscription: "What is past is prologue." In other words, history influences and sets the context for the present.[100] Israel's history and church history have proven time and again that God's people have a tendency to "mingle with the nations and learn their ways" (Psalm 106:35). In other words, as Tommy Nelson says, they "trim their sails to the prevailing winds of culture," forsake their spiritual roots, and fall into idolatry, apostasy, and sin.[101] In our day, we've witnessed the gradual erosion of our basic scriptural foundations. Like the frog in the kettle with the heat slowly rising, we sit by and slowly roast in the pot.

Culture influences belief, but Scripture alone should influence our spiritual beliefs. Culture is relative, while Scripture is constant. Yet we've allowed cultural trends to modify our spiritual values over and over again. In the 18th century, for example, the Enlightenment changed the way many people viewed the teachings of Scripture. The reason of man became more important that the revelation of God. Science and philosophy were elevated over Scripture. Modern liberalism with its corrosive effect on the church is the offspring of the Enlightenment.[102] And there are many such "ism's" that have invaded and polluted the church through the years. Learn from the past, because "evil men and imposters will proceed from bad to worse, deceiving and being deceived. You, however, continue in the things you have learned and become convinced of. . ." (2 Tim. 3:13-14a, NASB).

8. Ministry

*A*ccording to Ephesians 4:11-13, Jesus intends for the ordinary folks of the church to be equipped by church leaders to do the work of *ministry*. But what *work* are they equipped to do? Doesn't conventional wisdom dictate that the professionals do the *real* work of ministry? Everyone else's primary role is to attend the services, give money, and get along. The passive environment of the modern church service is the model of ministry, right? We sit quietly in long rows, stare at the backs of other heads, and listen to one guy do all the talking. Oh yes, and we get to sing a little too! Is that it? Does our role involve little more than learning a few helpful hints on how to live better and have a nice day? Don't the *ministers* do the ministry, and the *members* get ministered to?

In fact, ministry is service to God through work or labor for the good of others, or that is helpful to others.[103] Ephesians 4:12-16 shows that the primary goal of ministry (in the Greek, *diakonia*) is to build a unified body of mature, complete disciples. And it's the saints, the ordinary folks of the church, that are the main players in accomplishing this mission. (I'll explore this role in detail in Chapters 9 and 10.) In Chapter 3, I briefly discussed church ministry dynamics, stating that Jesus raises up spiritual leaders of various gifting and function to equip the saints to do the work of ministry (Eph. 4:11-12). Thus, we may rightly conclude that *all* Christians are called, and in fact, gifted for ministry. From the most menial of tasks to the greatest of spiritual accomplishments, ministry comes in many shapes and forms. From the offering of a cup of cold water to the ultimate sacrifice of life itself, everything we do can be in service to our Lord and his kingdom.

Vocation/Profession

I went to law school, in part, because I believed the golden rule, that people should be treated fairly and act justly. I naively thought that lawyers sought to advocate justice for *all*. It wasn't until I was in law practice that I learned how much the *other* golden rule controlled their actions and motivations, where "them that's got the gold makes the rules." Lawyers are famous for their ability to manipulate people and circumstances for personal financial gain, or spin the truth to achieve the desired result. And many cloak themselves in a self-righteous banner of truth, justice, and the American way. It's the reason their popularity is so high! But it's not just lawyers. How many businessmen, doctors, politicians, professors, servicemen, government employees, and others live primarily to advance their own careers and success, even at the expense of others. Models of service? Hardly. Is it realistic to think that Christians can serve God in their jobs as legitimate ministry? Yes! Every business and every calling is a ministry or *diakonia* if its labor benefits others.

Somewhere along the way, we divided the *secular* from the *sacred*, a distinction God does not make. We act one way when engaged in the sacred, and another in pursuit of the secular, because of course the rules are different for each. So the Christian who lives the same way in both circumstances has a rare testimony. The true test of a man may be how *sacred* he acts in matters considered *secular*. Consider men like Joseph and Daniel, highly intelligent and extremely talented, propelled into world-class leadership positions. These men maintained their integrity and acted consistent with their values in all circumstances, even when it cost them dearly. Can we rightly consider their jobs as ministry? Their credibility was a powerful witness. God clearly put them in significant roles in pagan governments where they honored God by their service. And that's the most important aspect of any ministry—God's honor (1 Cor. 10:31). God can be honored in any legitimate work, whether the job's great or small, and whether it involves running the country, preaching the gospel, or cleaning commodes.

But why do we have to work? Well first, we work in order to eat and thus to live. Through honest, gainful employment, we meet our own needs by serving others. And God created work to be good. It existed from the beginning before the fall in the garden of Eden, where God directed Adam to cultivate and keep the garden (Gen 2:15). After the fall, work became more difficult when God said, "Cursed is the ground because of you; in toil you will eat of it all the days of your life. . . . By the sweat of your face you will eat bread. . ." (Gen 3:17b, 19a, NASB). So now work is harder, but it's still good. Paul exhorts slaves (in modern times, employees) to serve with a sincere heart, not just with eye service (Col. 3:22). He advised them that even the most menial of tasks can honor God and serve Christ, stating:

> Whatever you do, do your work heartily, as for the Lord rather than for men, knowing that from the Lord you will receive the reward of the inheritance. It is the Lord Christ whom you serve (Col. 3:23-24, NASB).

It's been my experience that service-oriented work includes three distinct kinds of tasks: *welcome tasks, routine tasks,* and *unwelcome tasks. Welcome tasks* involve work that I'm motivated and skilled to do. I see the benefit to others, I'm good at it, and I'm excited to do it. *Routine tasks* seem to be many and ongoing. They're not particularly hard or exciting, but they need to be done on a regular basis. *Unwel-*

come tasks are tasks that I don't particularly want to do. They may be boring and monotonous, or they may be grueling and distasteful. But these are the ones that build and reveal character! Can I do them well with a good attitude, honoring God, and serving others?

Service involves all three. Just ask any mother. Her job and ministry to her children are among the most important on the planet. She shapes the next generation from their origin, and has many welcome tasks and memorable events. But she also has more than her fair share of unwelcome and routine tasks, including innumerable poopy diapers, dirty clothes, and food messes. And where would we all be without her? Her children rise up and call her blessed (Prov. 31:28)!

Certainly, we long to use our God-given talents in our work, and we'd like it to make a difference. Most of us have to work to meet our needs and provide for our families, but we'd like to find some fulfillment in our work as well. Given that we live in an imperfect world, can we find an occupation that allows us to excel in useful work that we love to do while making a decent living? I've found Jim Collins' Hedgehog Concept in *Good to Great* to be helpful in this regard. He postulates that at the intersection of three concentric circles there exists an integrated and unified vision for your vocational calling. First, you do work for which you have a God-given talent and can excel. Second, you're passionate about the work and love to do it. And third, you can make a good living doing it.[104]

Collins says that you need all three circles to have a well-developed Hedgehog Concept. You can't excel if you're not passionate about what you do. But your passion won't make up for an inability to excel at your chosen task. And you need to make a living, so it helps if you can combine the three or integrate them in your life vision. The Hedgehog Concept comes from Isaiah Berlin's famous essay, "The Hedgehog and the Fox," where he divided the world into hedgehogs and foxes, based on the ancient Greek parable that said the fox knows many things, but the hedgehog knows one big thing.[105]

Berlin said that foxes pursue many ends at the same time, and are scattered and diffused. They never integrate their thinking into one overall concept or unifying vision. Hedgehogs, however, simplify a complex world into a single organizing principle or concept that unifies and guides everything. Thus, anything that does not somehow relate to the hedgehog idea holds no relevance. The hedgehog sees what is essential and ignores the rest.[106] Recall how Billy Graham described the vision of Dawson Trotman, "This one thing I do, not these forty things I dabble in."[107] In Chapter 9, I'll discuss the role of *tentmakers* and the nature of a *fully integrated life*.

Spiritual Gifts and Service

Apart from the various natural talents useful in vocations, God has specially gifted his children with spiritual gifts to be used in concert to edify or build up the body of Christ. Before describing specific spiritual gifts in 1 Corinthians 12, Paul said:

> Now there are varieties of gifts, but the same Spirit. And there are varieties of ministries, and the same Lord. There are varieties of effects, but the same God who works all things in all persons. But to each one is given the manifestation of the Spirit for the common good (1 Cor. 12:4-7, NASB).

Much like the diverse instruments of an orchestra, the various spiritual gifts work in unison to build a unified body of *complete disciples*.

The varieties of gifts generally fall into one of two categories, the *speaking gifts* and the *serving gifts* (1 Peter 4:10-11; Rom. 12:6-8; 1 Cor. 12:8-10). Their purpose is to serve the body and glorify God. "Each one should use whatever gift he has received to serve others, faithfully administering God's grace in its various forms" (1 Peter 4:10, NIV). The gifts, therefore, have a unity of *source* and *purpose*.[108] They're given sovereignly by the Spirit for the benefit of the body. And that's important to remember because we have a tendency to get proud because of our gifts and talents as though we're special or better than others, forgetting both their source and purpose. We also tend to exalt those with the speaking gifts over those with the serving gifts. But the one who humbly serves, whatever his gift, will be the greater in God's eyes.

The *types* and *nature* of spiritual gifts have been topics of much popular and scholarly Christian literature, surveys, inventories, and gift tests.[109] Therefore, I won't spend time discussing these aspects of the gifts. Rather, I'd like to address the *use* and *stewardship* of spiritual gifts, topics that receive less attention. To do so, I want to focus on applicable principles in Jesus' parable of the talents (Matt. 25:14-30) and parable of the minas (Luke 19:11-27). Although they differ in certain respects, these two parables have a number of similarities. In each parable, the master entrusts his slaves with a significant amount of money, and expressly or impliedly tells them to engage in business until he returns. He expects them to do business with his resources while he's gone, with apparent freedom to decide where to invest.

They're using the boss' resources to do business and gain a profit for him upon his return. And he will reward them according to their *faithfulness*. It also appears that losing the initial investment was not a possibility because even the two failures could have at least deposited the money in the bank (money lenders in that day) and earned simple interest. So there wasn't really a down side to this deal, although the two errant slaves seem to have thought otherwise. As with spiritual gifts, there was both a unity of source and of purpose in the stewardship entrusted to the servants. In the parable of the talents, the slaves were given differing amounts, and the investments of the faithful slaves yielded corresponding profits. In the parable of the minas, the slaves were given equal amounts, but the investments of the faithful slaves yielded different profits.

The difference in the profits, however, appears to be secondary to the main point of the parables, and described simply to show that God gives gifts to his people as he sovereignly chooses. The central point of both parables is the *faithfulness* of the slaves with the stewardship entrusted to them. The degree of *fruitfulness* was secondary. The real issue was whether they would be about the master's business while he was gone, seeking to multiply his investments, or whether they would offer a lame excuse for why they did nothing with the gifts entrusted to them. What the master wanted to see upon his return was profit, growth, increase, expansion — *critical mass*! And losing was not even an option. Every faithful servant was a winner!

We need to be careful to avoid legalism here, but we don't generally think about spiritual gifts as a stewardship. We see them more as Christmas presents to play with as long as they amuse us. But that was not Paul's perspective. He saw them as a stewardship of God's grace, given to him for the benefit of others (Eph. 3:2, 7). "For if I do this voluntarily, I have a reward; but if against my will, I have a stewardship entrusted to me" (1 Cor. 9:17, NASB). In reality, God has entrusted his vast and precious resources to us for multiplying his investments to his glory.

He wants to see a critical mass of growth in the body of Christ, and he's far more interested in the expansion of his kingdom than we can possibly imagine! He's not asking us to do something with nothing. We start with a staggering amount of resources that he's entrusted with us to invest in his "business" for his "profit." We therefore have the high privilege of being involved in the greatest enterprise of all time! Think about it. There's nothing that anyone has ever done or built or achieved or conquered that even comes close in significance to the eternal kingdom of God!

What could you possibly do with your life that in any way compares?

It's beyond incredible that men will waste their lives building sand castles that simply wash away with the tide, when they could be part of building the only thing that lasts and remains forever. And a second group is even more pitiful—those who have been entrusted with God's gifts and simply do nothing other than make excuses to cover their disobedience. It brings home the famous saying of American poet John Greenleaf Whittier. "For of all sad words of tongue or pen, the saddest are these: 'It might have been.'"

God expects his gifts to be put to good use, because they *will* yield a profit. As one commentator has said, "[i]n the Christian life we do not stand still. We use our gifts and make progress or we lose what we have."[110] Both parables conclude with this same lesson on stewardship. To him who has, more will be given, but from him who has not, even what he has will be taken away (Matt.25:29; Luke 19:26). Dr. William Barclay called this an "inexorable law of life" in his commentary of the parable of the minas, stating:

> If a man plays a game and goes on practicing at it, he will play it with even greater efficiency; if he does not practice, he will lose much of whatever knack and ability he has. If we discipline and train our bodies, they will grow ever fitter and stronger; if we do not, we will grow flabby and lose much of the strength we have. . . . There is no such thing as standing still in the Christian life. We either get more or lose what we have. We either advance to greater heights or slip back.[111]

Addressing this same stewardship lesson in his commentary of the parable of the talents, Dr. Barclay stated:

It lays down a rule of life which is universally true. It tells us that to him who has more will be given, and he who has not will lose even what he has. The meaning is this. If a man has a talent and exercises it, he is progressively able to do more with it. But, if he has a talent and fails to exercise it, he will inevitably lose it. If we have some proficiency at a game or an art, if we some gift for doing something, the more we exercise that proficiency and that gift, the harder the work and the bigger the task we will be able to tackle. Whereas, if we fail to use it, we lose it. . . . It is the lesson of life that the only way to keep a gift is to use it in the service of God and in the service of our fellow-men.[112]

Did you catch that Dr. Barclay's explanations of the "inexorable law of life" and "universal rule of life" were descriptions of *critical mass*?

We need to discuss one more aspect of this stewardship. Recall that the master empowered and commissioned his servants to their purpose. Therefore, should the spiritual leaders of the church, as the delegated under-shepherds of the body of Christ, actively *empower* and *commission* others in ministries appropriate to their giftedness? Mark Day did just that for me when I became a leader in the Navigator college ministry at Texas A&M. Blake Purcell, the previous campus director, was led to move to Russia in 1990, and he asked me to take over the ministry. I was overwhelmed at first, but he left anyway! Mark Day was the regional Navigator Staff leader over all the Texas campuses, and fortunately for me, he lived in College Station.

Mark went out of his way to empower and enable me to run the ministry and experiment with different ideas and approaches. I'm quite certain that without his willingness to let me lead and encouragement to utilize my gifts, I would not have done so. I was still a full-time attorney with three young children, serving in the ministry part time. As far as I knew at the time, I was the only part-time staffer in the U.S. ministry that was allowed to run a significant campus ministry. Mark recognized my gifts, and enabled me to lead the ministry. I don't know that anyone else would have let me do it. He wasn't hung up on convention or tradition. He simply wanted to turn us loose to minister according to our gifting. And if we were faithful, we got all the opportunities we could handle!

Because of Mark, I was able to speak and teach regularly, organize and run Bible studies, weekly fellowships, and weekend and week-long retreats and conferences. I had more fun using every creative idea I could muster to reach and disciple college students in large group, small group, and one-to-one settings. I gained invaluable experience that I might never have gained otherwise. Mark was that rare leader who thought outside the box, and put *function* over *form*, instead of the other way around. He was my greatest advocate, and I loved working for him. But I also needed reigning in from time to time, and Mark was faithful to do that too. I remember once asking him if I had the potential to lead at a higher level. He readily affirmed my skill, but graciously advised that what I *really* needed to develop was the character and wisdom to go along with it! Would that more spiritual leaders empower their folks to develop and use their spiritual gifts for the good of others!

Disciplemaking

At the apex of ministry is *disciplemaking*. If the central goal of the Christian life is Christlikeness, then the central mission of Christian ministry is disciplemaking or helping others become like Christ. Matthew records at the end of his Gospel that the eleven remaining disciples were gathered around Jesus at the mountain in Galilee after the resurrection. He charged them with the greatest of all missions, which we call "the Great Commission." His commission had one primary command, *make disciples*, accompanied by three participles, *going, baptizing,* and *teaching* (Matt. 28:18-20).[113] He wanted them to make disciples among all the nations of the earth, both in going to them and as they went through life. As part of the process, new disciples were to be baptized, which is the final step of evangelism in publicly identifying with the body of Christ. And new disciples were to be taught to put into practice and live out everything Jesus commanded. In other words, they were to be discipled by more mature disciples.

For many years, it was believed by some that this commission applied only to those first eleven guys. Generational growth will just happen on its own, right? Well, Jesus said that he was *with them* until the end of the age, and the age hasn't ended, but the first disciples are long gone. Did the second generation make disciples, and did that continue on from generation to generation? Of course! We should rightly conclude that the Great Commission applies to Christians of *all* generations until the close of the age. I will address the details of disciplemaking in Chapter 10, spiritual leadership in Chapter 11, and spiritual multiplication in Chapter 12. But for now, let's simply describe *disciplemaking* as the process of developing *complete disciples,* including both the ministries of *evangelism* and *discipleship.*

There are many good and useful ministries within the body of Christ, but none is more important than disciplemaking. Many important ministries are what I'll call *two-dimensional* in effect. That is to say, they are completed with the execution or delivery of some form of service to others. We deliver food to the poor or aid to the weak. We sing in the choir, take up the offering, work in the nursery, teach a Sunday school class, lead a small group, or deliver the Sunday message. Certainly these are ongoing, needed, and valuable ministries, but they're essentially complete when the service itself is rendered. Thus, they are two-dimensional in nature — *cause* and *effect.* All members of the body are gifted and called to render these and many other such services for the general edification of others.

Disciplemaking, however, is on another plane entirely. It's what I'll call a *three-dimensional* ministry. One who disciples another to maturity and fruitfulness in Christ is actively participating in the Great Commission. When we pour out our lives to invest in others and help them grow, we're fulfilling God's desire to build a magnificent and eternal kingdom, full of people made complete in Jesus' likeness, reflecting the beauty and glory of God. This is the highest calling and ultimate purpose of ministry! In parenting, when we train our children to be mature, responsible adults, they in turn, will be equipped to start their own family and raise their own children. The same is true in disciplemaking. When we spiritually reproduce and develop mature disciples, they will be able to do the same across generations. Thus, it's three-dimensional in nature — *cause, effect,* and *chain reaction.* All two-dimensional ministries support and are subordinate to this one! And I can't say it strongly enough — the ministry of disciplemaking is God's mechanism for *critical mass* in the church.

But is everyone called to disciplemaking? Lorne Sanny used to say that for a growing disciple to catch the vision and start making disciples himself was like breaking the sound barrier. He receives help for a time and is committed to following Jesus, and then one day he finally turns to face the next generation, having caught the vision for reaching and discipling others. He willingly takes on the mantle of a disciplemaker. Some break through the sound barrier and others never seem to get there. It's a mystery to me, although I know of two main reasons why it occurs. First, many people are content to *receive* with no concept of *giving.* They're driven by a consumer mentality, and focus on what they get out of church, not what they give back or pass on to others. Second, they fight insecurity, thinking that they have nothing to offer, or that they're simply not good enough.

131

But you only have to be a few steps ahead of the ones you're helping, and you don't have to know it all just to get started.

Let's take a look at the church body make-up by analogy. Will it be normative for most adult Christians to get married and have children? Of course, there are many exceptions, but by and large most adults will marry and have a family, raising their own children. At the same time, they will likely work in an occupation of their choosing within their skill set. Their occupations will vary, just as their spiritual gifts vary, but their families may look fairly similar. So, is it normative for most married adult believers to raise children while they work at their particular occupations? Sure it is. Therefore, should it be normative for most Christians to make disciples a few at a time, while they exercise their broader spiritual gifts for the good of the body? Of course, and that includes the discipling of their own children.

Let me address one final issue at the core of disciple-making, and that's a genuine *heart for the lost*. Without exception, all of us were lost and without Christ at some point in our lives. And yet we quickly lose interest in others in the same position. I'm no exception. I find it so easy to get caught up in my "Christian work" and forget about those who need it most. But Jesus came to seek and to save the lost (Luke 19:10; Matt. 18:11). In fact, there is more joy in heaven over one sinner who repents than for 99 righteous persons who need no repentance (Luke 15:7). Jesus sought out, readily received, and regularly related to the lost because he was driven by a genuine love for people, especially for the outcasts and the unlovable. He had compassion for people who were distressed and dispirited like sheep without a shepherd (Matt. 9:36). He promised soul-rest for the weary and heavy-laden (Matt. 11:28-29).

But what's my default attitude toward the lost? I'm more like the sons of thunder (James and John), who upon experiencing the rejection of a Samarian village while traveling with Jesus, asked if they should call in a strategic missile strike (Luke 9:54)! If that's how they want to act, then let's consume them with fire! But Jesus rebuked them soundly, reminding them that he'd come to save men's lives, not destroy them (Luke 9:55-56). He didn't want men to perish, but to have eternal life (John 3:16). And that means putting up with a lot of mess, because people are messy! I should expect people to act lost if they are lost, and it's pretty ugly at times. So can I see them as God sees them, and love them as God loves them? I *cannot* of myself, but God's Spirit in me certainly can!

III.

Citizen Soldiers

9. Tentmakers

C itizen soldiers are first *tentmakers*, which has come to mean Christians engaged in ministry from some occupational platform other than full-time, vocational Christian work. While it generally refers to an overseas missionary who enters a country as something other than a missionary, i.e. an English teacher, engineer, or doctor, there's no reason that all Christians everywhere should live as anything other than tentmakers. Jesus has called us out of the world and sent us back into it to live out the truth of the gospel. The term *tentmaker*, therefore, is a metaphor for a lay Christian who integrates his occupation and ministry.

To address this topic, let's begin with a little church history on the involvement of ordinary saints in ministry. Philip Schaff in his multi-volume *History of the Christian Church* concluded that, among other things, the Protestant Reformation restored three foundational truths to the church. The first was *sola fide*. Salvation is by faith alone in the finished work of Christ on the cross, earned by no human effort. The second was *sola scriptura*. The Bible is the supreme and final authority in faith and life. No human being has authority equal to or superior to the word of God. The third was the *priesthood of all believers*. Every believer may approach God directly in Christ, and none of us need a human mediator. The veil into the holy of holies is forever torn open. Every believer is a priest before God and to other men.[114]

Yet, when it comes to ministry, we have not fully realized this last truth. Most of the work of ministry is still carried out by professionals—full-time Christian workers or ministers. And that was never God's plan. That's the equivalent of having the head football coach run all the plays and make all the tackles. We wonder why so many of our pastors burn out or quit the ministry. The whole team is supposed to play the game, with each player fulfilling his role, and the coaches doing their part to train, motivate, and lead the team.

A Second Reformation

Theologian John Stott once said that "the first reformation put the *Bible* in the hands of laymen; the second reformation will place the *ministry* in the hands of laymen."[115] Ministry in the hands of laymen—is that a scary thought? How could the professionals control it? Movements are like that! And yet, as Ford Madison used to say, the church can't hire enough people to do the job it's been called to, and in reality 99% of all Christians will live and minister in the ordinary working world. Think of that fact for a moment: 99% of all Christians *won't* be professionals. So does that mean they're all excused from ministry, and little more than cheering fans for the few hardy souls talented and tough enough to play professionally? Certainly not!

Remember, the ordinary people — the saints — the citizen soldiers do the work of the ministry, according to Ephesians 4:12. The professionals and leaders equip the saints, but the saints are the *heart* of the ministry. They're the team that wins the game! And the game's out there in the everyday working world and in the market place. So the 99% of us need to quit thinking like spectators and start living like tentmakers!

In Paul's day, a literal *tentmaker* was a skilled craftsman who worked in leather and *cilicium*—cloth woven from long-haired black goats used by armies, caravans, and nomads.

Paul had both a *trade* as a tentmaker and a *profession* as a rabbi (minister, teacher, lawyer — all in one), and later as an apostle. It was proper for a rabbi to practice a manual occupation so as not to profit from his spiritual teaching. Thus, it was a rule among the Jews that every young man, whatever his profession, should also learn a trade as a resource in time of need. In theory, no rabbi took fees, but supported himself. So before becoming a master in Israel, Paul had to master a trade.[116]

At times as an apostle, Paul was a self-supporting missionary, and provided for his entire staff. At the same time, he taught publicly and from house-to-house. His lifestyle was an example to others, and established credibility for his ministry. He worked hard like the people he reached, but devoted his free time to ministry. At other times, he also received financial support from various churches. Paul purposefully modeled a **fully integrated lifestyle** of vocation and ministry. Let's look at a few passages:

> Paul went to see them (*Aquila and Priscilla in Corinth*), and because he was a *tentmaker* as they were, he stayed and worked with them. Every Sabbath he reasoned in the synagogue, trying to persuade Jews and Greeks (Acts 18:2b-4, NIV, note and emphasis added).

While in Corinth, Paul worked at a regular job in his friends' business during the week and ministered on the weekends. In his last visit with the Ephesian elders, Paul summarized his ministry and lifestyle as follows:

> You know that I have not hesitated to preach anything that would be helpful to you but have taught you publicly and from house to house. . . . You yourselves know that these hands of mine have supplied my own needs

and the needs of my companions. (Acts 20:20, 34, NIV).

Paul made it a point to remind them that he worked to supply his own needs and also the needs of his staff. And he did it to pull his weight, maintain his credibility, and set an example for others. He made the same points twice to the Thessalonians:

> Surely you remember, brothers, our toil and hardship; we worked night and day in order not to be a burden to anyone while we preached the gospel of God to you (1 Thess. 2:9, NIV).

> For you yourselves know how you ought to follow our example. We were not idle when we were with you, nor did we eat anyone's food without paying for it. On the contrary, we worked night and day, laboring and toiling so that we would not be a burden to any of you. We did this, not because we do not have the right to such help, but in order to make ourselves a model for you to follow (2 Thess. 3:7-9, NIV).

Paul often worked to support himself and even his staff as a literal tentmaker, but let's remember that he also said that those who proclaim the gospel should make their living from the gospel (1 Cor. 9:14). So I'm not trying to down-play vocational ministry. On the contrary, I'm trying to show the absolute necessity and validity of lay and *tentmaking* ministry. Paul set an example that he intended the 99% to emulate. Today, we think of a tentmaker as a self-supported missionary, or a missionary who enters a country through some other vocation. But I think it's appropriate for all ordinary Christians *not* in full-time vocational ministry to think and live like tentmakers. The implications of such a lifestyle are far reaching.

Building the Wall

Nehemiah was the last great, godly leader of the Old Testament. He was not a professional minister, but a layman who had risen to the post of trusted advisor to the king of a foreign land, much like Joseph and Daniel. In about 444 B.C., he took on the impossible task of rebuilding the wall around Jerusalem, and in the face of intense opposition from without and abuse from within, he completed the work in a mere 52 days (Neh. 6:15). Even his enemies recognized that the work had been completed by the help of God (Neh. 6:16). A little background puts the enormity of this project into perspective. The northern kingdom of Israel was taken into captivity by Assyria in 722 B.C. In 586 B.C., the southern kingdom of Judah was taken into captivity by Babylon who destroyed Solomon's temple and tore down the walls around Jerusalem. Zerubbabel lead the first exiles back to Judah in 538 B.C., and the temple was rebuilt in 515 B.C. Ezra led a second group back in 458 B.C., and led a reform among the people.

Nehemiah led the third and last return to Judah in 444 B.C., to rebuild the wall of Jerusalem and its social structure. Despite his comfortable Persian government job, he became burdened by the state of his homeland and people. The wall was broken down and the gates were burned with fire. So he prayed for a season, repenting on behalf of Israel, reminding God of his promise to restore the nation, and asking for favor before the king. He put his neck on the line and stepped out in faith, boldly asking the king for permission to rebuild the wall, and for construction materials plus a military escort for safe passage. Miraculously, the king granted all his requests, and he went to Jerusalem to scout out the scene, plan the project, and recruit the people and local leaders for the work. Meanwhile, he had to fight off the direct and indirect opposition to the work by Israel's enemies. So, Nehemiah was both *building* and *battling*, which is at the heart of every ministry.

Chapters 3 and 4 of the Book of Nehemiah record that God used the leadership of Nehemiah and other local leaders, along with the coordinated efforts of priests, Levites, tradesmen, merchants, families, and neighbors from other regions in rebuilding the wall. In other words, the clergy, the professionals, the missionaries, and especially the large number of local and out-of-town laymen worked together to build the wall! And it's fair to conclude that without the involvement of the laymen, the job could not have been completed. Everyone pulled their weight and built their section of the wall, and together they rebuilt the wall.

> Eliashib the high priest and his fellow priests went to work and rebuilt the Sheep Gate. . . . The men of Jericho built the adjoining section, and Zaccur son of Imri built next to them.
>
> The Fish Gate was rebuilt by the sons of Hassenaah. . . . Meremoth son of Uriah, the son of Hakkoz, repaired the next section. Next to him Meshullam son of Berekiah. . . made repairs, and next to him Zadok son of Baana also made repairs. The next section was repaired by the men of Tekoa,. . .
>
> . . . Next to them, repairs were made by men from Gibeon and Mizpah. . . Uzziel son of Harhaiah, one of the goldsmiths, repaired the next section; and Hananiah, one of the perfume-makers, made repairs next to that. . . . Adjoining this, Jedaiah son of Harumaph made repairs opposite his house, and Hattush son of Hashabneiah made repairs next to him. Malkijah son of Harim and Has-

shub son of Pahath-Moab repaired another
section and the Tower of the Ovens. Shallum
son of Hallohesh, ruler of a half-district of
Jerusalem, repaired the next section with the
help of his daughters. (Neh. 3:1-12, NIV).

This description goes on for 32 verses in Chapter 3,
naming the workers and describing the portions of the
wall they built, and highlights the importance of everyone
pulling their weight to get the job done. And while I can't
pronounce most of their names, God recorded them in
Scripture along with their specific contributions. I'll add
a few final references to highlight the diversity of the
workers involved:

The repairs next to him were made by the
priests from the surrounding region. Beyond
them, Benjamin and Hasshub made repairs
in front of their house; and next to them,
Azariah son of Maaseiah. . . made repairs
beside his house. . . . [A]nd between the
room above the corner and the Sheep Gate
the goldsmiths and merchants made repairs.
(Neh. 3:22-23, 32, NIV).

In chapter 4, Nehemiah recorded his observation about
the work: "So we built the wall and the whole wall was
joined together to half its height, for the people had a mind
to work" (Neh. 4:6, NASB). The significance of their col-
lective achievement should not be lost, and serves as an
example today. "For whatever was written in earlier times
was written for our instruction" (Romans 15:4, NASB).
Meanwhile, Israel's enemies plotted to stop the work by
terrifying and discouraging the workers, then by attacking
and killing them. But Nehemiah found out about their
schemes and reorganized the workers so that half the men
did the work while the other half protected them from

attack (Neh. 4:16-17). They were building and battling at the same time. "As for the builders, each wore his sword girded at his side as he built. . ." (Neh. 4:18, NASB).

The work of building was never performed in a vacuum, always in the midst of a battlefield, and so it is with all ministry carried on by the citizen soldiers of the church. They are *building* and *battling* as they labor to advance the kingdom of God in the lives of men! Only now the work is comprised of living stones. "As you come to him, the living Stone — rejected by men but chosen by God and precious to him — you also, like living stones, are being built into a spiritual house to be a holy priesthood, offering spiritual sacrifices acceptable to God through Jesus Christ" (1 Peter 2:4, NIV).

A Legacy of Citizen Soldiers

Since the time of the American Revolution, America has always relied on its citizen soldiers to carry the weight of the country's defense. While our professionally-trained officers and soldiers are second to none, they would not have accomplished their mission apart from the massive involvement of the citizenry. And in many cases, some of the country's most successful military leaders were not professionals, starting with our first commander-in-chief, George Washington.

As to his primary occupation, he was first and foremost a farmer. As a younger man he'd been a surveyor, and later a volunteer aide to British General Edward Braddock during the French and Indian War. He had no formal schooling and certainly no formal military training. Noted author Bruce Catton described him as one of six great men of the Revolutionary era (from a worldly perspective), along with Benjamin Franklin, John Adams, Thomas Jefferson, James Madison, and Alexander Hamilton. Other notable founding fathers included Patrick Henry, Samuel Adams, George Mason, Richard Henry Lee, and others. But Washington is in a class by himself. How is it among so many distinguished founders that George Washington alone is called *the* father of our country? What did he do that set him apart from all the others?[117]

Soon after he was named the commander-in-chief of the fledgling Continental Army, he saw gathering against him the largest expeditionary force of the 18th century. Among the thirty thousand troops fighting for the British army — the greatest army of its day — were ten thousand Hessian mercenaries. The British and Hessian troops were well trained, while the American troops were little more than amateur soldiers. The fact is that Washington's army never defeated the main British army in open battle. They were defeated time and again, except for morale-boosting victories at the outposts of Trenton and Princeton. Recall the drama of the Delaware River crossing on Christmas night in 1776.[118]

Like Washington, his closest and most reliable senior officers were citizen soldiers. Henry Knox, his brilliant artillery chief, was a Boston bookseller. Nathanael Greene, perhaps the brightest of Washington's generals, was a Rhode Island foundryman. Both Knox and Greene were almost entirely self-educated. Joseph Reed, Washington's secretary, was a Philadelphia attorney. Among his other generals, John Thomas was a Massachusetts physician. William Heath was a fifth-generation Connecticut farmer, and John Sullivan was an attorney and politician from New Hampshire.[119]

European military observers compared the ragged American army to swashbuckling brigands. Another European officer, Von Closen, wrote more seriously, "It is incredible that soldiers composed of men of every age, even of children of fifteen, of whites and blacks, almost naked, unpaid, and rather poorly fed, can march so well and stand fire so steadfastly." He credited their discipline to Washington, and observed that he was "admirable as the leader of his army, in which everyone regards him as his father and friend."[120]

In the end, this rag-tag band of citizen soldiers outlasted the most powerful army in the world primarily due to the perseverance of its commander-in-chief. Military historians have long debated Washington's ability as a soldier. Some contend that he was incompetent as a supreme commander, while others have compared him to Caesar and Napoleon. As Washington historian, James Flexner, observed, the "debate has always overlooked the fact that Washington was never really a soldier. He was a *civilian in arms.*"[121]

But Washington held the army together, and gave it spirit through its most desperate times. David McCullough, author of *1776*, said that above all else, "Washington never forgot what was at stake and he never gave up." "He was not a brilliant strategist or tactician, not a gifted orator, not an intellectual." He made serious mistakes and showed marked indecisiveness at crucial times, but he learned from experience, and he simply *persevered* more than anyone else in the Continental Army or Congress. McCullough concluded that "[w]ithout Washington's leadership and unrelenting perseverance, the revolution almost certainly would have failed."[122]

In his Pulitzer Prize winning biography of Washington, Ron Chernow summarized Washington's leadership as follows:

> His fortitude in keeping the impoverished Continental Army intact was a major historic accomplishment. It always stood on the brink of dissolution, and Washington was the one figure who kept it together, the spiritual and managerial genius of the whole enterprise: he had been resilient in the face of every setback, courageous in the face of every danger.
>
> . . .
>
> As Benjamin Franklin told an English friend after the war, "An *American planter* was chosen by us to command our troops and continued during the whole war. This man

sent home to you, one after another, five of
your best generals, baffled, their heads bare
of laurels, disgraced even in the opinion of
their employers."[123]

And *that* is why George Washington is *the* father of our
country!

Fast forward two centuries to the time of World War II
when Army Chief of Staff George C. Marshall transformed
the U. S. Army from 170,000 men in 1940 into an army of 7.2
million three years later. Historian Stephen Ambrose said
it "was the best equipped, most mobile, with the most firepower, of any army on earth. This achievement was one of
the greatest accomplishments in the history of the Republic."
What they attempted in 1944 had never been done before—
a massive invasion of France, the largest amphibious invasion in history. It was the largest American army of citizen
soldiers ever assembled, with the fate of the world resting
on its shoulders. And there was no historic precedent for
what they were about to do.[124]

In his popular book, *Band of Brothers*, Ambrose chron-
icled the men of Easy Company of the 506th Parachute
Infantry Regiment, 101st Airborne Division. On the morning
of D-Day, in its first combat action, they captured and put
out of action a German artillery battery looking down on
Utah Beach. The men of E Company came from different
backgrounds and different parts of the country.

> They were farmers and coal miners, moun-
> tain men and sons of the Deep South. Some
> were desperately poor, others from the
> middle class. One came from Harvard, one
> from Yale, a couple from UCLA. Only one
> was from the Old Army, only a few came
> from the National Guard or Reserves. *They
> were citizen soldiers.*[125]

As a result of their shared experiences, these men experienced a closeness unknown to outsiders. They had complete trust in each other, and as comrades, they were closer than friends or brothers.[126]

Ambrose summarized their invaluable service after D-Day to the close of the war as follows:

> The company led the way into Carentan, fought in Holland, held the perimeter at Bastogne, led the counteroffensive in the Battle of the Bulge, fought in the Rhineland campaign, and took Hitler's Eagle's Nest at Berchtesgarden. It had taken almost 150 casualties. At the peak of its effectiveness, in Holland in October 1944 and in the Ardennes in January 1945, it was as good a rifle company as there was in the world. The job completed, the company disbanded, the men went home.[127]

And the greatest citizen soldier of them all was their commander, Dick Winters. Openly friendly and somewhat reserved, he was genuinely interested in his men and their training. He led by example, not by fear, and his men loved and trusted him. Winters got his men to perform because he expected nothing less than their best, and they didn't want to let him down. He grew up in Lancaster, Pennsylvania, where his family attended the Reformed Church. He put himself through college at Franklin & Marshall during the Great Depression, graduating in the spring of 1941. He was inducted into the army that August and later became an infantry paratrooper and officer.[128] His first combat was on D-Day, June 6, 1944. At the end of that fateful day, he wrote in his diary, "I did not forget to get on my knees and thank God for helping me to live through this day and ask for his help on D plus one."[129]

Four months after D-Day on October 5, 1944, Dick Winters and Easy Company showed why they were among the best light infantry outfits in the Army. With only 35 men, Winters and a platoon routed two German SS companies of about 300 men in Holland near a crossroads at a dike. Finding his platoon surrounded while on patrol, Winters led them on a 200 yard sprint across an open field to attack the larger German force. Having realized his men could not safely withdraw, and not wanting to retreat anyway, he attacked against ten-to-one odds. "God give me strength," Winters prayed, and led out ahead of his men to reach the dike first. He climbed the hill and began firing from the hip *by himself* into the confused German flank, emptying multiple clips before his men caught up with him. It's the bravest thing I've ever heard a soldier do! But "follow me" was his code, and he took more risks and fought harder than anyone else.[130]

Winters later refused to take any credit for himself, but called this fight the highlight for the entire war and the best single day in Easy Company's history, even better than D-Day, because it demonstrated the company's "overall superiority in every phase of infantry tactics." His men were just as proud of him, writing to him after the war:

> Dick, you are loved and will never be forgotten by any soldier that ever served under you or I should say with you because that is the way you led. You are to me the greatest soldier I could ever hope to meet.
>
> . . .
>
> You were blessed (some would say rewarded) with the uniform respect and admiration of 120 soldiers, essentially *civilians in uniform*, who would have followed you to certain death.[131]

A Fully Integrated Life

In citing Paul's life as a literal and spiritual tentmaker, Nehemiah's team efforts to rebuild the wall of Jerusalem, and America's citizen soldiers in battle, I've tried to make the case for the indispensible role of modern tentmakers in the church. They are the citizen soldiers of ministry, without which there is no effective or wide-spread disciplemaking ministry. But in order to reach the battlefield, they must learn to successfully integrate and balance the four main areas of life — *personal, family, work,* and *ministry,* or they will succumb to the tyranny of the urgent.

Men in particular have a difficult time balancing their priorities. Work often takes precedence over everything else, and for several reasons. Men find their significance in work, and it can become an obsession or idol. We also feel the pressure to provide for our families and measure up to our employers', clients', or customers' expectations. The crush of modern life and the state of technology press us to perform faster and longer. The world has become more complex, which also directly affects our modern work life. Our jobs demand a large portion of our time and effort, and most men are simply too tired to do much else after work except watch television. Wives are neglected; kids are neglected; and ministry may consist of little more than sporadic church attendance. Such is the prevailing American lifestyle.

Is it possible in the modern world for a Christian man to do excellent work within reasonable boundaries? It depends on what he's living for, and it depends on his focus, commitment, and discipline. Does he love God above all else and is he willing to sacrifice to seek first the kingdom of God? If so, then yes he can live as a tentmaker — a *citizen soldier.* A man's true priorities are shown by the choices he makes in the use of his time. If he loves God, he'll set aside regular time to spend in the word and prayer. If he loves his family, he will spend time with them. If he wants to be meaningfully involved in ministry, he will make time for it. He won't let work take all his time and energy. He learns to work hard for reasonable periods of time, and then leave it to pursue other priorities. No man ever lay on his death bed wishing he'd spent more time at the office! He laments the time he didn't spend with his family. He doesn't regret his lack of financial investments. He regrets his lack of eternal investments.

But the fact remains that it's difficult to balance the various demands and responsibilities of life. If we cave to fear or pleasure, work becomes slavery or idolatry. I'm ever more convinced that balance in life is only attainable through an abiding relationship with Christ and continued trust in God's provision. You can't do it on your own. No one can. And yet through Jesus we are more than conquerors (Rom. 8:37). Set your priorities with an eternal perspective in mind, and learn to say "no" to the opportunities that come your way when they don't fit in with your *priorities*. Sometimes, *good things* can be the chief enemy of the *best things*. There's nothing particularly wrong with good things, except when they keep us from the best things. We have a limited supply of time and energy, and we want to make it count!

Years ago, my long-time mentor and friend, Ford Madison, shared with me his habit of keeping an index card divided into four parts with the priorities and goals he'd set for each of the four main areas of his life—*personal, family, work*, and *ministry*. He wanted to stay on track and growing, and had kept a card like this for years. Did I mention that he was 65 when he first showed me his index card? I piggy-backed his idea and later drafted a purpose statement for each of these four areas of my life. I recommend the practice. It's helped me focus my priorities and refine my goals. I also learned to count the cost of discipleship. If I really intended to be involved in discipling men and committed to ministry, I'd have to forgo the American dream of "fame and fortune" as a lawyer. In fact, early on I had to forfeit a partnership position in my law firm to protect the time I committed to leading a college discipleship ministry. It had a significant impact on my earnings at the time, but God honored it and I concur with Jim Elliot's famous quote: "He is no fool who gives what he cannot keep to gain that which he cannot lose."[132]

I know many good Christian men who excel at work and love their families, but are content to stay on the sidelines of ministry. This can result from a weak spiritual walk. The men who by personal conviction and sacrifice find a way to excel at work, family, and ministry are rare. To maintain such balance, as well as a strong walk with God and quality time with family, is the *ultimate* challenge in modern Christian life. Yet, it's not uncommon for laymen gifted in ministry to feel a pull to full-time Christian work, and for many it's the right move. Others feel outside pressure to change vocations, whether directly or indirectly from a legalistic sentiment that if they're truly committed, they'll go "full-time." But since every Christian is a priest with a calling to ministry, the choice of vocation is person specific. And let's remember that 99% of all Christians are laymen. In many respects, it's more difficult and challenging to work in the business or professional world, maintaining credibility in the marketplace, and at the same time disciple men in an active ministry.

No one has done it better than Ford Madison. He's among the greatest citizen soldiers of our age, and he is to the American church what Dick Winters was to the American army. Ford became a believer in his mid-twenties while a young businessman in Colorado Springs in the 1950's, and was discipled by Bob Foster and Lorne Sanny. He married Barbara, his high school sweetheart from Amarillo, and they had five children, all of whom are active Christians with their own families. It would be difficult to count the number of lives he's impacted over more than 50 years of discipleship ministry. He is a patriarch in the truest sense (*see* Chapter 12), but he's also a successful businessman in commercial real estate, and has served on numerous Christian boards, including Dallas Theological Seminary, The

Navigators, and the English Language Institute—China. But he does the latter because he's such a gifted leader. His real passion has always been one-to-one and small group discipleship.

He found his life's direction in 1 Corinthians 7:20-24. Stay in the calling in which you were called, Paul instructs. The slaves addressed in these verses, he reasoned, could be compared with today's employees. Paul said, in effect, "don't worry about the condition you were in when you became a Christian, but if you can be made free, do it." Ford pondered verse 21 and asked himself what such freedom would look like. If he was self-employed and financially independent, freedom would mean the ability to go anywhere in the world that God would send him to disciple men. He then set out to earn his freedom, and did! He's traveled all over the world, and lived in the Philippines, Nicaragua, Kansas, and Texas, as a self-supported tentmaker, actively involved in disciplemaking.

I've never known anyone with such a passion for equipping laymen to be lifetime disciplemakers, and he brings such credibility to the table because he's done it himself for so long. Mind you, he once was asked by Ray Stedman to be the discipleship pastor at Peninsula Bible Church in California, and by Billy Graham to be the director of The Cove in North Carolina. Ford has world class talent as a leader and businessman, but he's stayed true to his calling to disciple men from a tentmaker's platform, balancing the demands of work, family, and ministry. And I'm one of the many who have been greatly blessed by his spiritual investment. While most of us don't have his talent or business acumen (I certainly don't), we can emulate his tentmaking model of one-to-one and small group discipleship ministry. It's never been the flashy, big-event style ministry that motivated him, but the faithful, low profile discipleship resulting in spiritual multiplication that mattered.

10. Laborers

*I*f *citizen soldiers* serve from an integrated platform as *tent-makers*, then their primary ministry role is that of *laborers*. Used as a metaphor, a *laborer* (or *worker*) is a front-line disciplemaker, a harvest worker, a fisher of men, a builder of people. But a laborer has no status, no rank, and no prestige. His ministry is largely unheralded and unrewarded this side of eternity. He is a common field hand, a private foot soldier, a mere servant, and few at that. His job is slow, messy, costly, and sometimes richly rewarding. A laborer is a spiritual parent, loving and training his children. He is a mentor, challenging and motivating his protégés. And his ministry is the *greatest* calling in the church!

In other words, a *laborer* makes disciples, investing in people and building them up to maturity and fruitfulness in Christ. He is something more than an ordinary disciple. He meets with men individually (life-to-life) and in small groups. He's involved in reaching people for Christ, but doesn't stop there. He trains disciples, but doesn't stop there either. His job is not done until his men are mature, fruitful disciples, and reproducing disciplemakers themselves. He is, in fact, the principal human change agent for the promotion of *critical mass*!

The Path to Christlikeness

One of the best and simplest illustrations I've seen to describe the process of disciplemaking was created and used by Ford Madison. (See illustration below.) The essence of a discipling relationship involves a mature disciple who comes alongside a younger disciple, and helps him take the next step or steps on the path to Christlikeness. Likewise, personal evangelism involves a Christian coming alongside a non-Christian and helping him take the next step or steps toward faith in Christ.

I used to think it was my sole responsibility to take a person from A to Z in his spiritual life from spiritual birth to maturity. But the reality is that I don't control how long I'll walk alongside another guy or whether he'll respond and grow according to my expectations. In fact, God will likely use a number of people to lead a person to faith or disciple a young Christian. That was certainly my experience. My parents were most influential in my early spiritual development. After college, four men in particular made significant spiritual investments in my life. As a discipler myself, I learned long ago that my job is to be *faithful*. God controls the degree of *fruitfulness*.

The Path to Christlikeness

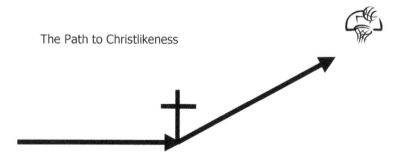

If the goal of the Christian life is Christlikeness in every area of life, then a laborer comes alongside a young disciple to help him take the next steps on the path to that goal. After salvation, progress should be gradually uphill, although it may fluctuate on the uphill climb. Whether a laborer comes alongside another guy this side of the cross or along the uphill path, his goal is either to help the other guy take the next steps toward faith in Christ or in becoming like Christ.

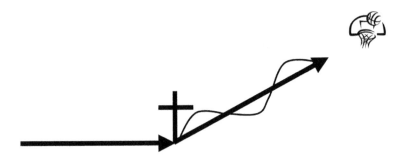

A laborer, therefore, pours himself into the lives of others, ministering to both *foundational needs* and *felt needs*. *Foundational needs* are those areas of life that we all need to grow in, including the five areas of a *complete disciple*. We all need to be grounded in the Word and grow in our devotion to Christ. We all need to pursue holiness, address sin, and develop the fruits of the Spirit. We all need to build strong relationships, learn the major doctrines of the faith, and develop our spiritual gifts to minister to others. *Felt needs* are those issues unique to each person, such as character deficiencies (i.e. anger, lust, or pride), relational struggles (i.e. parents, spouse, or children), emotional weaknesses (i.e. fears, anxieties, or failures), and the like. People have all manner of special needs, especially in our day of countless broken families and collapsing societal values.

Both Jesus and Paul demonstrated the heart and ministry of a laborer. Jesus began his ministry of proclaiming the gospel by meeting extreme personal needs, but he also taught vigorously the foundations of spiritual growth. He repeatedly taught the same gospel truths to different groups of people, but he also ministered to the special needs of individuals. As he traveled around, he was moved with compassion for the people he saw to be weary, scattered, and leaderless. He challenged his disciples to pray that God would send out laborers into the harvest of needy souls. "The harvest is plentiful, but the *laborers* are few," he said (Matt. 9:35-38). His twelve disciples became the first such laborers after he gave them authority, named them apostles (or special representatives), and sent them on their first short-term mission trip (Matt. 10).

In like manner, Paul said, "The man who plants and the man who waters have one purpose, and each will be rewarded according to his *labor*. For we are God's *fellow workers (laborers)*; you are God's field, God's building" (1 Cor. 3:8-9, NIV emphasis added). That *one purpose* for which they labored was that every person be made complete in Christ (Col. 1:28-29). In fact, Paul boasted more than once that he *labored* by the grace of God more than anyone else! (*See* 1 Cor. 15:9-10; 2 Cor. 11:23.)

While in prison, he shared his radical ministry vision with the Philippians: "For to me, to live is Christ and to die is gain. But if I am to live on in the flesh, this will mean *fruitful labor* for me" (Phil. 1:21-22, NASB emphasis added). He then confessed his internal struggle between the desire to go home and be with the Lord versus their need for his continued ministry (Phil. 1:23-24). Convinced that it was in their best interest that he stay, he said "I know that I will remain and continue with you all for your *progress and joy* in the faith," (Phil. 1:25, NASB emphasis added). Their continued spiritual growth was Paul's number one objective! Their progress on the path to Christlikeness was his goal. And even the joys of heaven calling from a dank prison cell could not keep him from it!

But it's important to remember that laboring involves both *felt* needs and *foundational* needs. You will likely begin a discipling relationship by meeting the felt needs of another because they're often the most urgent, and left unaddressed can hinder spiritual progress. However, if we only minister to felt needs, then we may do little more than provide spiritual "ER" care, which can inadvertently cater to self-centeredness. On the other hand, you don't take a crippled person to the gym and start working him out, or you may cause irreparable injury. You first help him through a season of healing or therapy before getting him into the gym. There needs to be a balance in discipling others in both felt needs and foundational needs in order to promote real spiritual progress.

Spiritual Parenting

Laborers invest in people the same way parents invest in their children. As Paul expressed to the Thessalonians, "Having so fond an affection for you, we were well-pleased to impart to you not only the gospel of God but also our own lives, because you had become very dear to us" (1 Thess. 2:8, NASB). He didn't just give them a simple message and move on. He loved them and poured his life into them. He compared his ministry to the care of a nursing mother, the integrity of a tentmaking brother, and the discipline of an exhorting father (1 Thess. 2:7-11).

> But we proved to be gentle among you, as a nursing mother tenderly cares for her own children (1 Thess. 2:7, NASB).

> For you recall, brethren, our labor and hardship, how working night and day so as not to be a burden to any of you, we proclaimed to you the gospel of God. You are witnesses, and so is God, how devoutly and uprightly and blamelessly we behaved toward you believers; just as you know how we were exhorting and encouraging and imploring each one of you as a father would his own children, (1 Thess. 2:9-11, NASB).

After describing the nature of his roles, Paul concluded with the goal of his ministry: "so that you would walk in a manner worthy of the God who calls you into His own kingdom and glory" (1 Thess. 2:12, NASB). In a balanced ministry exhibiting the traits of a caring mother, a tent-making brother, and an exhorting father, Paul demonstrates his commitment to their maturity and God-given destiny. Each of these roles is critical to an effective disciplemaking ministry. (We've already discussed the role of a tentmaker who pulls his weight in Chapter 9.)

An imbalanced or lopsided ministry will not develop complete, well-rounded disciples. A ministry dominated by "nursing mothers" may focus on felt needs to the neglect of foundational needs. Likewise, a ministry dominated by "exhorting fathers" may concentrate on foundational needs and ignore felt needs. Just as God provided in the family, we need the influence of both our spiritual "mothers" and "fathers." Children raised in single-parent homes often suffer the emotional and developmental consequences from a lack of the other parent. We need a lot of encouragement and support, but we also need to be challenged and held accountable. We need spiritual fathers to speak into our lives and address the hard issues, but we also need the comfort and compassion of spiritual mothers.

But let's be more specific. A laborer is a disciplemaker, a mentor, a coach, and a friend. He invests in people, and pours his life into them. Disciplemaking is relational but intentional, and more an *organic* process than an *organizational* program. By that I mean it's less a formal curriculum than it is an apprentice relationship utilizing the "*with him*" principle from Mark 3:14, where Jesus chose the twelve that they might be with him. In his seminal book on disciplemaking, *The Master Plan of Evangelism*, Dr. Robert Coleman points out that the essence of Jesus' training program was simply to let his disciples follow him:

When one stops to think of it, this was an incredibly simple way of doing it. Jesus had no formal school, no seminaries, no outlined course of study, no periodic membership classes in which he enrolled his followers. None of these highly organized procedures considered so necessary today entered into his ministry. Amazing as it may seem, all Jesus did to teach these men his way was to draw them close to himself. He was his own school and curriculum.

The natural informality of this teaching method of Jesus stood in striking contrast to the formal, almost scholastic procedures of the scribes. These religious teachers insisted on their disciples adhering strictly to certain rituals and formulas of knowledge which distinguished them from others; whereas Jesus asked only that his disciples follow him.[133]

Dr. Coleman also observed:

The time which Jesus invested in these few disciples was so much more by comparison to that given to others that it can only be regarded as a deliberate strategy. He actually spent more time with his disciples than with everybody else in the world put together. He ate with them, slept with them, and talked with them for the most part of his entire active ministry. They walked together along the lonely roads; they visited together in the crowded cities; they sailed and fished together on the Sea of Galilee; they prayed together in the deserts and in the mountains; and they worshiped together in the synagogues and in the Temple.[134]

While Jesus was ministering to others, his disciples were with him. When Jesus addressed the multitudes, spoke to a lonely beggar on the road, or sparred with the scribes and Pharisees, his disciples were nearby, observing and listening. In this way, his ministry paid double dividends. In other words, he was *establishing* them in the faith, but also *equipping* them for ministry. As a result, Dr. Coleman rightly concludes that Jesus' disciples got the benefit of everything he said and did to others, along with their own personal explanation and counsel. They clamored for his attention like sons to a father, and he wanted them with him. "They were his spiritual children, and the only way that a father can properly raise a family is to be with it."[135]

The Organic Process

While the discipling process is more *organic* than *organizational*, it does involve certain key steps in promoting the mature development of disciples. Lorne Sanny wisely advised that you take who God gives you, start where they are, and see how far you can go. There are many strategies used to recruit and disciple guys, but the strategy I've most often used, and the one that has been used by the men who discipled me, was a bi-focal approach employing a combination small group and life-to-life strategy. I've used this strategy for many years in college ministry, men's groups, and small groups. Essentially, I began by recruiting a few key guys to a discipleship-oriented Bible study, and encouraged them to recruit some other guys. The group might range from 5 to 20 guys.

We'd meet regularly at my house for several hours a week, and would often do a basic spiritual leadership and character study of Saul, Jonathan, and David from 1st Samuel, or of Joshua and Caleb from the book of Joshua. We've also studied the life and ministry of Jesus from one of the gospels, or study one of Paul's epistles. My initial goal was to get them regularly in the Bible, studying the lives of godly men, and learning to apply the word of God to their lives. Along the way, I'm observing them to gauge how spiritually hungry they are in order to fish out a few of them to go deeper and disciple life-to-life. It's a simple and straightforward strategy, but I've seen it work many times.

Most notably, Ford Madison has used a similar strategy for years. For almost twenty years since he moved to College Station, Ford has taught a college Sunday school class at his church on biblical principles applied to life after college. It's a basic but relevant topic for students nearing graduation. His higher goal, however, was to fish out a few students in his class to disciple life-to-life. I can't begin to count the number of lives he's impacted in just the years I've known him, and I've seen him use the same strategy with local coaches involved in a Coaches' Outreach ministry small group.

Although we're prone to think that the big events have the greatest impact, it's really the faithful, consistent investment in a few people at a time over a long period of time that yields the greatest results. The discipleship small group provides an entry-to-intermediate level discipleship experience, while the life-to-life relationship provides an opportunity for advanced training and development. On a number of occasions, I've also discipled guys I've met apart from a small group study. And on other occasions, my life-to-life meetings have been with more than one guy at a time. Where several guys are interested in life-to-life discipleship and already have a close friendship with each other, I've met with them one-on-two or as many as one-on-three. As a general rule, though, I've reserved life-to-life discipling relationships for spiritually-hungry men who show both an appetite and an aptitude for something more that the routine or ordinary.

The life-to-life discipling process can be described in different ways, but from my study and experience, I've learned that it involves at least the following key steps: *choosing, diagnosing, training,* and *launching.*

Choosing. Care is exercised in the selection of a person to disciple. Not every Christian values the opportunity to be discipled or particularly wants the personal investment. Only the squeaky wheel gets the grease. It takes time to get to know and evaluate a potential candidate before committing to disciple him. A discipler is looking for a teachable, God-hungry person to invest his life in. He's looking for a committed, faithful man who will prepare and do his homework before they meet. As they used to say, he's looking for a "FAT" boy, a guy who is faithful, available, and teachable. He's looking for a man after his own heart, in other words, a man he can relate to and connect with.

And it doesn't take tricks or gimmicks to get him to respond. He's like a cat on the back screen door. Every time you go out the back door, he's clawed to the screen, wanting your attention, hungry to grow! He's got the passion and commitment to make it worth your time. Just as a financial investor doesn't want to waste his money on a bad stock or mutual fund, a laborer doesn't want to waste his time on a lukewarm Christian. There's too many of them as it is, and the laborer's job is too important. He wants his investment to count, and he wants to promote real growth! This is not a hobby or a past-time, it's the *big job!* There's no more important ministry in the church than making disciples of Jesus Christ and building the kingdom of God.

In the mid 1990's, I met regularly with a young man who later became the top Corps leader at A&M. At the start of his senior year, Matt and I decided to recruit a group of his friends to be part of a Corps leadership Bible study. That group turned out to be a high-octane crew of senior leaders in the Corps. Among them was Bobby, who began noticing that Matt and I spent extra time together in a life-to-life discipling relationship. He showed up at my law office one day to tell me that he wanted what Matt was getting! And I told him, he would get it, because squeaky wheels always get the grease! Bobby was exactly the kind of guy I looked for, and we met regularly for the next several years until he left for the Air Force. I didn't even have to fish him out of the group. He jumped in the boat!

Diagnosing. After choosing a man to disciple, the laborer spends some time diagnosing him to determine where to start. Not every disciple needs to start at square one. This is not a disciple-by-the-numbers exercise. It takes some time to determine where he is along the path. There are many good discipleship materials out there to utilize in training a young disciple, but he doesn't need to repeat things he already knows. Some years ago, I discipled a fellow lawyer who had served for many years as an adult Sunday school teacher at his church. He didn't need to be grounded in the basics of the faith. But what I learned after spending some time with him was that he didn't have a regular quiet time, consisting of quality time in the word and prayer. He knew the basic doctrines of the faith, he just didn't spend regular time with God. And again, the simplest things are the most profound. Learning to have a regular quiet time or devotional time radically changed his life.

My goal is to find out where a guy is spiritually, and then design a discipleship program to fit his development needs. It's not unlike a doctor's role in taking a medical history from a patient and diagnosing his condition before prescribing a course of treatment. It's an intentional, relational process. But the person being discipled is not a *project* — he's a person! And people are discipled in the context of relationship the same way that children are raised in the context of family. We want to help them develop as complete disciples, but it takes time to find out a person's development needs. Remember, you're trying to help them take the next step or steps in the process of becoming like Christ in every part of their lives.

In the late 1990's, while leading a discipleship Bible study with a group of cadets, I got a call from a new graduate student who wanted to participate in a discipleship group. Greg was a West Point grad, and the Army had sent him to A&M to get a Master's degree. He participated in and helped lead the group study, but I also designed some advanced training for him. He was older than the other students, and married with three kids. But he wanted to be discipled and trained to disciple others. So he and I covered advanced material in our life-to-life time beyond what I covered with the other guys in the group, even the few that I met with life-to-life. He needed a greater challenge.

In an effort to promote a balanced and well-rounded growth, I look for areas of existing maturity and those areas that need attention. For example, some people have strong relational skills, but lack a scriptural foundation in the essentials of the faith. Therefore, we need to work on the latter, and spend less time on the former. Others have a strong biblical foundation, but lack mature relational skills or struggle with important character issues like anger or lust. Everyone is different, which makes an accurate diagnosis a crucial step in the discipling process.

Training. Now we're down to brass tacks—what do you actually do with the one you're discipling? *Regularity* of meeting is perhaps the most essential element. As my old friend Rob Holt used to say, "showing up" is half the battle, and really it's half the experience. There is no substitute for a consistent investment of *time*. Discipleship doesn't happen overnight; it happens over time. And it needs to be regular, not sporadic. I recommend weekly, or no less than bi-weekly, meetings of one to two hours each, over a period of one to three years. If you really expect to make a difference in another person's life, you must faithfully invest the time!

Every young disciple needs a combination of two things in life-to-life meetings— *encouragement* and *accountability*. He needs a lot of encouraging motivation, but he also needs basic accountability to follow through and address issues, and he probably needs them in a three-to-one ratio. That is, you need to lean heavier on the encouragement side. We all need a combination of positive and negative motivation, with about three times as much encouragement as accountability. We're in the ministry of building up men, and part of that involves speaking into their lives about areas of sin and other weaknesses that we observe to hinder their spiritual progress. But we need to speak the truth in love (Eph. 4:15).

I usually spend the first portion of my life-to-life time with a guy catching up on his life and the things going on in his world. I share the same with him. After that, I focus on the *content* of our training or study time. We may go through a book on a particular topic, or a book of the Bible, or cover other specific spiritual topics in the Bible. I draw from a number of "tools" in my spiritual tool chest, depending on the issues we're trying to address. There's been no other time in church history when so many resources are available to train people in the different areas of spiritual maturity. That's one reason I go back to my one-page blueprint of the Complete Disciple. It serves as my road map for the key areas of spiritual growth. Whatever the resource, I use it to address one of the five critical areas on my blueprint. In this way, I stay intentional in my training. I'm always working at building *complete disciples*.

Everything I do by way of content relates to one of the areas of devotion, character, relationships, doctrine, or ministry. And I can't say it enough—the simplest things are the most profound. Helping a person develop a consistent time in the word and prayer is the most important habit I can help him develop. So, we'll talk about his quiet time as part of our meeting, not every time, but from time to time. We'll discuss what he does, and what he's learning and experiencing from it. We'll also review verses we've memorized and meditate on. I remain convinced that God will speak to us through his word if we'll take the time to abide in it. And prayer fosters dependence on God and submission to his will. The word and prayer *will* transform a person over time.

I won't try to list all the resources available to use in training disciples in different areas of the Christian life or the five main areas of a complete disciple. There's too many to list, and I'm trying to focus on the *vision* for disciplemaking, more than the *tools*. A person is *not* discipled simply because he went through some training materials. From my observations, many people have gone through highly organized and comprehensive discipleship programs and studies, and not really experience the transformation that follows true, organic discipleship. The fact is that we should be able to use the Bible as our primary source to disciple others if we know it ourselves. However, there are many useful tools and resources to assist in the process.

Another important element of training is *preparation*. You must be prepared by having studied the content or materials to be discussed at your life-to-life meeting. You must stay ahead of the man you're discipling and know your stuff. Just as important, however, is that you set a standard for the person you're discipling to follow. You should expect him to prepare and do his homework before each meeting, and he should write it down. Although life-to-life time is highly relational, there should also be an expectation that your man study the material and be prepared to discuss it. If he is habitually unprepared or tardy for your meetings, then he isn't committed enough to warrant your regular investment of time. I don't mean to sound harsh on this issue, but you want a man who Dawson Trotman would describe as "down to business" and serious about his spiritual life. True passion will show itself in faithfulness.

Finally, one of the last important elements of training involves the laborer's ability to pass on the *vision* for both discipleship and disciplemaking. Your goal is to influence a man's way of life and way of thinking. Every time you meet, you want to be casting the vision for following Christ and building his kingdom—bringing every thought into captivity, transforming every part of life, and being caught up in the greatest mission on earth! You want to see him grow to maturity, but you ultimately want to see him become what you are—a laborer.

And it takes a long time for him to own that vision. Lorne Sanny used to say that becoming a laborer was like breaking the sound barrier. There's some mystery involved in who breaks through, and many don't seem to get there. It takes about three years on average for a growing disciple to get the vision (if he does), and then take on the *mantle* of laborer — to move beyond thinking like a kid to thinking like an adult, and then to move beyond just thinking like an adult to thinking like a parent! He has to hear it and see it over and over again, and then maybe, just maybe, he'll get the vision! The harvest is plentiful, but the laborers remain few.

Launching. When the man you're discipling gets the vision, and burns with motivation to get in the game, then it's time to work towards launching him into his own disciplemaking ministry. Lay it on his heart to look for a man to disciple, and help him get started. We'll talk more about coaching new disciplemakers and the attendant spiritual multiplication in the next two chapters. But the natural, last step in the discipling process is to kick the birds out of the nest and watch them fly on their own! You don't want them to be inordinately dependent on you for an indefinite period of time. They certainly will remain dependent on the Lord throughout their lives, but you don't want them to develop an unhealthy reliance on *you* so that you can feel good about yourself.

Sometimes, it's hard to let our own kids go. We get used to having them around, and sadden when they grow up too fast, and prepare to leave for college or a job. I've lived through this three times myself. My two sons have graduated from college, married, moved away, and started their own lives and families. My daughter will soon finish college and go out into the world. But our goal from the beginning was to see then grow up and become mature, functioning adults. As they grow up, we help them transition into the real world, and we want them to be able to stand on their own feet. If they remain dependent on us well into adulthood, then we've failed in some respects as parents. So too with the people we disciple. We want them to have a mature walk with God, to spiritually feed themselves, and to carry out their own ministry.

You might remember that Jesus launched his disciples into their disciplemaking ministry after three years of training. In a rather dramatic mountain setting, Jesus commissioned them in Matthew 28:18-20 (NASB), saying:

> "All authority has been given to Me in heaven and on earth. Go therefore and make disciples of all the nations, baptizing them in the name of the Father and the Son and the Holy Spirit, teaching them to observe all that I commanded you; and lo, I am with you always, even to the end of the age."

No Better Job, No Greater Sacrifice

Several times in his letters, Paul commends his fellow workers who have faithfully labored alongside him in the ministry. He also refers to them as brothers and sisters, fellow servants and soldiers, but conspicuous in his letters are the number of times he refers to them as *fellow workers* (*laborers*). We know very little about most of these men and women, and the label "worker" is not a particularly flattering term at first blush. But I think Paul means for it to carry a great deal of weight and honor. In Romans 16, he concludes his letter with a number of greetings:

> Greet Priscilla and Aquila (the original tent-makers), my *fellow workers* in Christ Jesus. They risked their lives for me. Not only I but all the churches of the Gentiles are grateful to them.
> Greet Mary, who *worked* very hard for you.
> Greet Urbanus, our *fellow worker* in Christ,
> Greet Tryphena and Tryphosa, those women who *work* hard in the Lord.
> Greet my dear friend Persis, another woman who has *worked* very hard in the Lord.

Timothy, my *fellow worker*, sends his greeting to you, (Rom. 16:3, 6, 9, 12, 21, NIV, emphasis added).

In 1 Corinthians 3:9, Paul referred to himself and his staff as God's *fellow workers*. In 2 Corinthians 8:23, Paul refers to Titus as his partner and *fellow worker* among the Corinthians. In Philippians 2:25, Paul refers to Epaphroditus as his *fellow worker* and fellow soldier. In Philippians 4:3, he refers to Clement, several women, and a number of others as his *fellow workers*. In Colossians 4:10-11, Paul commends Aristarchus, Mark, and Jesus called Justus as the only Jews among his *fellow workers* for the kingdom of God. Later in verse 13, he vouches for the fact that Epaphras is *working* hard for those in Colosse, Laodicea, and Hierapolis, wrestling in prayer for them that they may stand firm in all the will of God, mature and fully assured. In verse 17, Paul tells Archippus to complete the *work* he has received in the Lord. In Philemon 2, Paul greets Philemon as his dear friend and *fellow worker*. Later in verse 24, he refers to Mark, Aristarchus, Demas, and Luke as his *fellow workers*. Finally, in 1 Thessalonians 3:2, Paul refers to Timothy as his brother and God's *fellow worker* in spreading the gospel of Christ.

I personally believe that the ministry of the laborer is the single most important job in the church. How's that for a pure dogmatic statement! It is the *big job*! Every other job involves or supports *this* job. And this job was given to the ordinary *citizen soldiers* of the church. The laborers are the FLT's, the front-line troopers of ministry! Without them, there is no *critical mass* in the church. They are the infantrymen of the church. The infantry is part of the combat arms portion of the army, along with the artillery and armor (tanks), etc. Without the combat arms, there is no army. An army also needs the combat support elements, including supply, ordinance, medical, transportation, etc. But if the only functioning parts of the army are its supporting elements, then there really is no army. By analogy, the church today is top heavy in its "combat support" elements. We have the finest resources and facilities in church history, but there are precious few soldiers serving in the "combat arms" elements of the church.

Why is that? Well, for starters, as soon as you become a laborer, you get a bulls eye from the enemy on your forehead because you just became a threat. And you will be shot at! Once you engage in the mother of all battles, so to speak, expect to pay a price. Ministry is messy, thankless, and time-consuming. It's also costly, inconvenient, and aggravating at times. Some of your men will quit on you halfway into the process. Others will turn on you along the way, and later oppose or ignore you. Still others will want you to think they're with you in battle, only to sneak off when the going gets tough. If you labor in the field, expect to get sunburned, sore, and worn out. Labor is hard by definition!

Yet, the laborer's reward is seeing the people he's discipled standing mature and complete in the presence of the Lord at his coming (1 Thess. 2:19-20; 2 Cor. 13:9, 11). And there is great joy in seeing the ones you've worked with grow and mature in the Lord. In fact, there's nothing like it! Just like there's no greater joy than seeing your children grow up and blossom before your eyes, there's nothing like the satisfaction in seeing the people you've loved and discipled going in the right direction, on their way to becoming everything the Lord desires.

Paul showed his laborer's heart in expressing his commitment to the Corinthians regardless of their response: "So I will very gladly spend for you everything I have and expend myself as well. If I love you more, will you love me less? Be that as it may, I have not been a burden to you" (2 Cor. 12:15-16a, NIV). Paul also made clear that the quality of each man's labor will be tested and revealed by fire on the last day. If it remains, the laborer will receive a reward. If his work is burned up, he will suffer loss, though he himself will be saved. (1 Cor. 3:13-15.) In other words, your labor matters to a degree you can't imagine!

11. Pathfinders

*T*he lack of strong *spiritual leadership* is perhaps the greatest problem facing the modern church. This is especially true of male leadership. Many men have either abdicated their God-given leadership roles, passively deferring to others including women, or they exercise leadership as cold businessmen at best and tyrants at worst. The old adage, "as the leaders go, so goes the nation," applies with greater force to the church. As the *spiritual leaders* go, so goes the church! The ministries of discipleship and disciplemaking require solid leadership, because leaders equip laborers to make complete disciples. The citizen soldiers must be trained and led in their mission! Lorne Sanny used to say that leaders bring vision, faith, and courage to a coordinated effort—vision to see what to do, faith to believe it can be done, and courage to persevere until it is done.[136]

More than any other single term used to describe spiritual leaders, Scripture calls them shepherds. The term "shepherd" came to be used in the Old Testament to describe Israel's leaders, including priests, nobles, and judges.[137] A leader is a shepherd of people in that he cares for them, protects them, and leads them in the right direction. David was a literal shepherd before becoming Israel's chief shepherd and king. Of his leadership over Israel, the psalmist said that "David shepherded them with integrity of heart; with skillful hands he led them" (Psalm 78:72, NIV). Ezekiel, on the other hand, spoke out against the shepherds of his day, looking forward to the day when the Messiah would shepherd his people (Ezek. 34). And of course, Jesus called himself the "good shepherd" (John 10:11, 14), revealing himself as the long-awaited supreme leader. Peter exhorted his fellow elders to shepherd the flock of God (1 Peter 5:2).

While the picture of a shepherd was a common metaphor in Biblical times, it's not as familiar today. We're just not around that many actual shepherds — those who tend sheep. In fact, some only see shepherds as mild-mannered background figures in the Christmas play. The modern equivalent of the Jewish shepherd in our culture, however, would be the American cowboy — those who tend cattle. From our western heritage, we're familiar with the old cattle drives where tough, sunburned men cared for their herds and protected them from predators and rustlers along the trail. Jewish shepherds were like that too, but the modern image of a cowboy doesn't necessarily equate with strong leadership. So I looked for another term with Scriptural roots and less baggage to describe a spiritual leader, and settled on the term *pathfinder*.

Paths of Righteousness

The most famous shepherding Scripture, of course, is King David's Psalm 23. "The LORD is my shepherd, I shall not want. . . . He guides me in the *paths of righteousness* for His name's sake" (Psalm 23:1, 3b, NASB, emphasis added). David's son, Solomon, speaking as a father in Proverbs 4:10-11 said, "Hear, my son, and accept my sayings and the years of your life will be many. I have directed you in the way of wisdom; I have led you in *upright paths*" (NASB, emphasis added). In later times through Isaiah, God warned Israel of its poor leadership, "O My people! Those who guide you lead you astray and confuse the direction of your *paths*" (Isaiah 3:12b, NASB, emphasis added). God then promised, "'I will lead the blind by a way they do not know, in *paths* they do not know I will guide them'"

(Isaiah 42:16a, NASB, emphasis added). God directs our *paths* when we trust him whole-heartedly and don't rely on ourselves (Prov. 3:5-6). His word is a lamp to our feet and a light to our *path* (Psalm 119:105).

A pathfinder is a leader and a guide in the right direction or on the proper path. He runs ahead and out front. Metaphorically, he is a spiritual guide and a teacher. The spiritual guides and leaders of a church are pathfinders (Eph. 4:11). In the previous chapter, I discussed the paths to Christ and to Christlikeness. Who is it that leads a ministry of evangelism and discipleship but a *pathfinder*? He's a leader of disciples—a disciplemaker himself and a maker of disciplemakers. He casts the vision and sets the pace. He moves the ministry forward and coaches the team to victory! He's a trailblazer, head coach, and field general, but let's just call him a *pathfinder*.

Think Daniel Boone and Kit Carson, famous pathfinders from the east coast to the mid-west and from the mid-west to the west coast, respectively. They and men like them led out across the unexplored wilderness to new lands, while others followed and settled there. Think Tom Landry and Lou Holtz, head coaches who recruited top players, built dynasties, and won championships. Think General Washington and General Lee, commanders who mobilized, trained, and led ordinary citizen soldiers in desperate battles against great odds and superior opponents.

Another reason I like the term *pathfinder* is its historic military connotation. Since we're using the term *citizen soldier* to describe ordinary lay disciplemakers in the church, we can draw a related analogy by use of the term *pathfinder*. Pathfinders were infantry paratroopers who dropped in behind enemy lines prior to an invasion by the main army. They first appeared in World War II and continue to serve in the military today. They're part of the airborne infantry units that precede the invasion by the main body of the army. The pathfinders drop in before even the airborne units to locate the drop zones and provide guidance for the main force.

Once the airborne units have jumped into enemy territory, the pathfinders rejoin their original units and fight as part of the airborne infantry.[138] In other words, they lead out, guide the troops, and fight with the army.

And that's what spiritual leaders should do—lead out, guide the troops, and fight with the army! They lead from the front, set the pace, and model what they want others to do. Paul said to the Corinthian Christians, "Follow my example, as I follow the example of Christ" (1 Cor. 11:1, NIV). He said to the Roman Christians, "I will not venture to speak of anything except what Christ has accomplished through me in leading the Gentiles to obey God by what I have said and done" (Rom. 15:18, NIV). Paul led by example, and was himself headed in the direction he called others to go. As discussed in the previous chapter, Paul held a strong conviction to continue with the Philippians for their progress and joy in the faith (Phil. 1:25). On this point, John MacArthur commented: "*Progress* pictures trail blazing so that an army can advance. Paul wanted to cut a new path for the Philippians to follow to victory. . ."[139]

In John Bunyan's classic tale, *Pilgrim's Progress*, young Christian sets out on a journey to the Celestial City. A man called Evangelist helps him find and stay on the right path, teaching him to follow God's word on his pilgrimage. But Christian strays early on, taking the wrong path, and Evangelist steps in to help him get back on "the good way." Evangelist later catches up with Christian on his journey to check on his progress and warn him of dangers ahead, encouraging him to persevere in his pilgrimage.[140] Christian, you see, was led on his hazardous journey through the worldly wilderness to the Celestial City by Evangelist, who served as his *pathfinder*.

Primary Roles

I've had the privilege over several years of being a guest teacher in the disciplemaking course required of Master of Divinity students at Southwestern Baptist Theological Seminary. I've always found it motivating to teach energetic young leaders who are sold-out to God and want to make a difference for the kingdom. They're not yet scarred or frustrated by the realities of life and ministry, and they're brimming with hope and optimism. In fact, it's been my experience that the best time to influence and disciple a person is between the ages of 20 and 35. During this time, the "cement" is still wet and moldable. After about age 35, the cement hardens, and a person's pathway becomes fairly fixed. Before age 20, solid foundations are established, but youth and immaturity often slow the progress. In the window between ages 20 to 35, however, a person can make the most spiritual progress, and growth may be exponential. That was certainly my personal experience, and I've seen it many times in the men I've discipled over the years.

In one of the classes, I would always ask a few key questions about their future leadership roles. Most of them intended to be pastors in a church after graduation. I would have them take a few minutes and jot down their answers to the following questions:

1. What do you see as your primary ministry roles?
2. How will you know if you're succeeding or moving forward?
3. What will your church see as your primary ministry roles?

I asked them to base their answers on Scripture and their church experiences. The questions generated an interesting discussion that covered, of course, the conventional duties of a church pastor—preaching, counseling, and administration.

While serving on my church's elder board or meeting with other elders and deacons, I've asked the same essential questions that I ask of seminary students. Elders and deacons are typically absorbed in church administration, management, and personnel issues, along with their share of member crises. They function more as a board of directors of a corporation than a board of elders of a church. The business of the church seems to dominate elder meetings and consume most of their attention. *Things* seem to take precedence over *people*. It's classic tyranny of the urgent!

Most pastors also function as spiritual emergency room doctors, dealing with their members' personal crises on a regular basis. This role in particular has a debilitating effect on pastors. But stack that on to their top three responsibilities, and you have burn-out looming much of the time. People's problems are exhausting, and we often expect too much of our pastors. That's why they leave the ministry in droves. Few can keep the pace it demands. The modern role of a senior pastor is like the twin roles of a general leading the troops into battle and a MASH doctor treating the wounded. The problem is that these functions occur on opposite ends of the battlefield. It's practically impossible to do both jobs well, and most pastors will tend to one role or the other, usually the latter.

Ephesians 4:12, however, shows that a primary role of spiritual leaders is to *equip* the members of the church to do the work of ministry. (Have I pointed that out before?) This is a *proactive* ministry—making disciples, training leaders, and advancing the kingdom of God. Yet, spiritual leaders find themselves mostly doing *reactive* ministry—addressing personal crises, handling administrative demands, and running church programs. I don't mean to minimize the latter, just to point out that they consume too much time. And since pastors spend an inordinate time dealing with people in trouble, their sermons are geared more to *victims in crisis* than *disciples in training*. As a result, sermons are often couched in what I'll term *victim theology*, rather than *victor theology*. The church body as a whole is overly coddled and rarely challenged!

Dave Kraft in his excellent book, *Leaders Who Last*, states that "[a] leader is a person on a journey and has the ability to attract others to join him on that journey." (He's a pathfinder!) One of his greatest challenges is deciding who to get involved with and how much time to invest in them. A leader has to learn to prioritize the kinds of people to invest in. Many leaders, especially senior pastors, are reactive rather than proactive with their time. Kraft says that there are four types of people with whom spiritual leaders spend their time: draining people, nice people, resourceful people, and trainable people.[141] I heartily agree with his categorization, but would label them *needy people, nice people, growing disciples*, and *emerging leaders*.

Spiritual leaders typically spend most of their time with nice people and needy people. Nice people are nice to be around and want attention, but they don't want to go anywhere or do much. Needy people are immersed in a variety of problems, and should rightly receive a great deal of help, but they are draining and sometimes never seem to get better. Growing disciples and emerging leaders, on the other hand, get less time from spiritual leaders, and generally demand less time, so they get overlooked. Yet, they are the ones who should get most of the attention of spiritual leaders.[142]

As Kraft points out, many pastors and other leaders gravitate to the hurting, draining, and time-consuming people because they (the spiritual leaders) need to be needed. In addition, leaders with strong mercy gifts have more difficulty actually leading than others do, and that describes a lot of pastors.[143] That's not to slight the fact that leaders need to care for hurting and needy people. But when they dominate a majority of the time of pastors and spiritual leaders, then growing disciples and emerging leaders suffer, along with the health and future of the church. Leaders should spend most of their time investing in those who will most benefit from their influence.

With so little time available to deeply invest in others, leaders must think strategically in determining who gets their focused attention. In an article entitled "Seven Habits of Highly Ineffective Leaders," a satire based on Steven Covey's popular book title, Kraft said of spiritual leaders:

1. They spend too much time *managing* and not enough time *leading*.
2. They spend too much time *counseling* the hurting people and not enough time *developing* [growing disciples and emerging leaders.]
3. They spend too much time *putting out fires* and not enough time *lighting fires*.
4. They spend too much time *doing* and not enough time *planning*.
5. They spend too much time *teaching the crowd* and not enough time *training the core*.
6. They spend too much time doing it *themselves* and not enough time doing it *through others*.
7. They make too many decisions based on *organizational politics* and too few decisions based on *biblical principles*.[144]

So back to my questions to the Southwestern seminary students. After discussing the conventional roles, hazards, and expectations of pastoral ministry, I challenge them to see their primary role as *head coaches* rather than *celebrity speakers*. Howard Hendricks said, "You can *impress* from a distance, but you *impact* up close."[145] Pastors and their churches tend to see the preaching of weekly sermons to large audiences as the most important goal of ministry. Pastors are viewed as the equivalent of ace pitchers on the team, whose primary job is to take the mound each week and "bring the heat." Certainly they need to "preach the word" as part of their solemn responsibilities before God (2 Tim. 4:2). But when they gain notoriety because they excel at public speaking, then they're likely to be treated as celebrities. If that happens, then their popularity sets them apart from other people in the church, the same way it does in our culture. And while celebrities can impress, they don't necessarily impact, especially if they become detached and self-absorbed. The church needs more leaders, not more celebrities.

Head coaches, on the other hand, equip the team to play the game. They motivate the players and coach them to victory. Because, to *equip* is to make fully ready or completely qualified for a specific purpose.[146] And that's a primary role of spiritual leaders! Coaches do a lot of speaking, but it's part of their greater role to train and lead the team to the championship. Head coaches succeed when their team succeeds. In other words, the focus of their efforts is not on how well *they* perform *per se*, but on how well their teams play. As Paul said to the Thessalonians after quelling his fear that his labor might have been in vain, "for now we really live, if you stand firm in the Lord" (1 Thess. 3:8, NASB). I recall hearing years ago that another prominent seminary found in a study that it had produced many fine teachers over the years, but had largely failed to train leaders. Leaders certainly teach as part of leading, but pure teachers don't necessarily lead.

The Proposal

So here's my proposal. The pastors, elders, deacons, and other spiritual leaders of a local church should start their own *pathfinders* group. It consists of men who are investing in other men, discipling and mentoring on a life-to-life or one-to-one basis, and who otherwise lead in their church as small group leaders, Sunday school teachers, men's group leaders, or in some service role. This group should function like a special ops group within the larger army. It's akin to an order within a larger organization, but not separate from it, similar to military pathfinders within the larger airborne corps. It must be part of the organic local body because its purpose is to cast the vision, model the ministry, and coach others to do the same. So it's not a group outside or alongside the local body. It *is* the leadership of the local body, functioning *within* the church and subject to its governance.

And here's the key component—each man in the group must be discipling at least one other man, *no exceptions*. This isn't a group of sports commentators who talk about the game. It's a group of player-coaches who first and foremost play the game! Now this requirement immediately causes a problem in your church, doesn't it? You have few if any men who disciple others or even know how. Add to that, few if any of the men in your church have been discipled themselves. Or you may say that your pastors don't get it, or your most influential leaders don't get it, and therefore, you don't have a unified leadership group committed to life-to-life disciplemaking. This is where you follow the advice of Brig. Gen. Theodore Roosevelt, Jr., son of the president. During the D-Day invasion of June 6, 1944, a number of American troops landed on Utah Beach, but it was the wrong beach. They became disorganized and confused as to their mission. Roosevelt set about reorganizing their inland assault, and became a legend for reportedly saying: *"We'll start the war from right here."*[147]

If you have few spiritual leaders who disciple other men, then start with the few you have and let the ministry grow organically over time, the same way a family does. Adam had no brothers, and Abraham had no kids until he was old. If you don't either, then you'll become a patriarch to future generations (*see* Chapter 12). It has to start somewhere! Be the pathfinder! If no one in your church has been discipled, then find a mentor to disciple you, and start the ball rolling yourself. You can't be a good father unless you've had a good father. You can't be an effective disciplemaker unless you've been discipled yourself. Some think you can start the process with seminars and conferences, but it doesn't work. An *organizational program* will not jump-start an *organic process*. It can supplement, but it cannot replace, and there are no short cuts. It starts with one barren man who believes God and sees his life multiplied, just like Abraham!

I've helped start several pathfinder groups, and I'll be the first to admit that it takes a lot of time and effort to gain traction, which can then be easily lost. But here's what we did, and there's no magic prescription. First, we met at least once a month, usually at my house to create a more personal environment. Second, we wanted to build *esprit de corps* among the leaders by continually casting the vision for discipleship. Third, we were committed to doing these three things in our time together: (1) mutual support and accountability in our personal lives, (2) sharing "war stories" of our experiences with men we're discipling, and (3) advanced training in the areas of disciplemaking and leadership through book and Bible studies.

I've worked up an inductive study called *The Apostle's Apprentice* that looks at Paul's *ministry philosophy and practice* from 1st Thessalonians, Philippians, Colossians, and 2nd Timothy in that chronological order. 1st Thessalonians was written in about 50 A.D. The other books were written about 12 to 15 years later, with 2nd Timothy written last. I use these four epistles in particular because they contain some of the best and most concise material on Paul's ministry philosophy and practice. We read it from the perspective of the apprentice or assistant to Paul (*i.e.* Timothy, Silas, or Titus) observing his ministry (much like a resident working under a doctor), rather than the recipient of the letter. Most of the time when we study the Epistles, we read them from the viewpoint of a recipient of the letters or as a distant observer looking for personally relevant points.

Here, instead, we want to observe Paul in action as a leader and disciplemaker, and observe ministry from his perspective. We're looking over his shoulder, watching him do the ministry, and asking the following questions:

1. What is *ministry* in Paul's view?
2. What is the goal and focus of his ministry?

3. What is he trying to accomplish?
4. What does he do and why?
5. What does he teach and how does he coach?

We're not trying to strictly exegete every verse *per se*, but pull out significant passages that address these questions as we write down our observations about Paul's ministry philosophy and practice.

I envision pathfinder groups to be like the chiefs and mighty men of Israel in the days of King David. Scripture records that all Israel came together, including the leaders and elders, to make David king (1 Chron. 11:1-3). The chiefs of David's mighty men "together with all Israel, gave his kingship strong support to extend it over the whole land, as the LORD had promised" (1 Chron. 11:10, NIV). Chapter 12 describes the leaders and warriors of Israel and the twelve tribes. Of the leaders of Issachar, Scripture makes two extremely important observations: they understood the times, and they knew what Israel should do (1 Chron. 12:32). Of the men of Zebulun, Scripture observes that they were experienced soldiers, prepared for battle, with an undivided loyalty to David (1 Chron. 12:33). Oh that God would give us men like that in the church today—leaders and soldiers who come together in strong support of the kingship of Jesus, committed to extending his kingdom over the whole land as God has promised!

Coaching Champions

Let me offer one last illustration that will tie into the final chapter of this book on spiritual multiplication, the lasting legacy of a leader. Paul was fond of using sports analogies to convey truths about the Christian life, discipleship, and spiritual leadership. Consider his statements in this regard:

> Do you not know that those who run in a race all run, but only one receives the prize?

Run in such a way that you may win (1 Cor. 9:24, NASB).

I press on toward the goal for the prize of the upward call of God in Christ Jesus (Phil. 3:14, NASB).

Everyone who competes in the games exercises self-control in all things. They then do it to receive a perishable wreath (crown), but we an imperishable (1 Cor. 9:25, NASB).

Also if anyone competes as an athlete, he does not win the prize unless he competes according to the rules (2 Tim. 2:5, NASB).

In like manner, a modern sports analogy serves to illustrate the principle of leadership development and spiritual multiplication found in 2 Timothy 2:2 (NASB), which states:

The things which you have heard from me in the presence of many witnesses, entrust these to faithful men who will be able to teach others also.

In this simple statement, Paul reveals the principle of spiritual multiplication—leaders train leaders who train leaders. Prospective spiritual leaders must possess two indispensable qualities, faithfulness or demonstrated reliability and the ability to teach or coach others. In other words, they must show proven character and servant leadership. Paul looked down the corridors of history with a third-generation perspective. His focus was not just on Timothy's development and influence, but he saw the development and influence of Timothy's faithful men, and the men after that to the third generation. Let me illustrate.

Football is played at the highest level in the NFL and the winner of the Super Bowl receives the Lombardi Trophy, named for Hall of Fame Coach, Vince Lombardi. Lombardi is widely regarded as one of the greatest football coaches in NFL history. In nine years with the Green Bay Packers, he won five NFL titles, and the first two Super Bowls. In those nine years, his Packers finished either first or second eight times, and that was after Green Bay had been a perennial loser for the previous ten years. Using those same players, he shaped and coached the most dominant team of the 1960s. Nine members of that team are in the Pro Football Hall of Fame.[148]

So how did Vince Lombardi become a champion coach? Was he simply a self-made man? Hardly. The first of his two main mentors was Jim Crowley, Lombardi's college coach at Fordham University. Sleepy Jim Crowley was the third winningest coach of the 1930s, himself a former All-American running back at Notre Dame.[149] While you may not remember his name, if you follow college football on television, then you've seen him often in the famous photograph inspired by this sports clip:

> Polo Grounds, New York, Oct. 18, 1924. Outlined against a blue-gray October sky, the Four Horsemen rode again. In dramatic lore they are known as Famine, Pestilence, Destruction and Death. These are only aliases. Their real names are Stuhldreyer, Miller, *Crowley*, and Layden. . .[150]

While the theology in this historic clip is a little shaky, Jim Crowley was the most dynamic of the Four Horsemen of Notre Dame, National Champions in 1924. A decade after leaving Notre Dame, he brought the legend of the Horsemen to Fordham where he coached Lombardi, who learned many coaching lessons from Crowley. Crowley, in turn, was coached by none other than Knute Rockne, among the greatest and most innovative college coaches of all time. Rockne won multiple national championships and put Notre Dame on the map as a national football power.[151]

Knute Rockne is the father of Notre Dame's long-winning tradition. He was called "a builder of spirit" for his ability to maintain enthusiasm among his men. He tried to remain close to his players, and encouraged them to consult him on personal issues. Many who played for him also became football coaches. In fact, Rockne's "most invaluable contribution to college football was the development of a whole colony of coaches." Rockne personally coached and launched into coaching 41 major college football coaches. "He was a teacher par excellence and reaped great enjoyment out of seeing his disciples move into the front ranks of the coaching field." Jim Crowley was one of them, and a true disciple of Rockne. Knute Rockne coached Jim Crowley, and Jim Crowley coached Vince Lombardi.[152]

But there's a second branch to Lombardi's coaching lineage. Before he became an NFL coach, Lombardi served as an assistant coach at West Point under the infamous Col. Red Blaik, the winningest college football coach of the 1940s. Blaik won two national championships and had two Heisman trophy winners, Davis and Blanchard — Mr. Inside and Mr. Outside. Lombardi once said that everything he learned about organizing a team and preparing it to play its best, he learned from Col. Blaik.[153]

Blaik's life-long mentor was Gen. Douglas MacArthur. MacArthur was the superintendent of West Point when Blaik was a student and football player, and took a keen interest in the football team. (In 1924, he told Blaik that if he'd stayed at West Point as superintendent, he intended to get Rockne as coach because "Army sorely needed aggressive leadership on the gridiron.") For years while Col. Blaik was the head coach at West Point, he regularly consulted and briefed Gen. MacArthur on the status and progress of the team. Col. Blaik adopted Gen. MacArthur's style of leadership and his most repeated quote: "*There is no substi-*

tute for victory!" Vince Lombardi also regularly quoted that statement to the Packers.[154]

On the stone portals of the West Point Gym is inscribed Gen. MacArthur's statement on the leadership-training value of football. "Upon the fields of friendly strife are sown seeds that upon other fields, on other days will bear the fruits of victory."[155] Gen. MacArthur mentored Red Blaik, and Red Blaik mentored Vince Lombardi. Great leaders build championship teams and train future leaders who build championship teams and train still more leaders to build championship teams — and thereby achieve *critical mass!*

12. Patriarchs

*M*ature, fruitful disciples spiritually reproduce as a normal part of their Christian lives. In fact, they reproduce reproducers, and thus over time become *spiritual patriarchs*. *Critical mass* results from the multiplying effect of spiritual reproduction, which gives disciplemaking its three-dimensional quality. Spiritual multiplication, therefore, is absolutely critical to the growth and future of the church. Without it, the church dies in a generation. So who are patriarchs? Abraham was the patriarch of Israel. David was the patriarch of Israel's kings. And Jesus, in a sense, is the greatest patriarch of them all, both as the founder of a people, the church, and the kingdom.

Every Christian—every Christ-one has been endowed by the Spirit to do the works of Jesus (John 14:12), and his work of building an eternal kingdom occurs through the spiritual multiplication of his followers (Matt. 28:18-20; John 17:18-21). The patriarchs of the church, therefore, are those who have labored to make disciples as a way of life, allowing God to multiply the life of Christ though their lives across generations. Patriarchs are ordinary Christians and full-time ministers, common laborers and gifted leaders that have been discipling others long enough to be spiritual grandparents and great-grandparents, influencing generations through their spiritual descendants long after they're gone.

Spiritual Multiplication

Spiritual multiplication is one of the most important, but least understood and least modeled doctrines in the Bible. From the first command of God in Genesis to the last command of Jesus in the Great Commission, the multiplication of godly offspring has been paramount. Recall the Bible's first recorded statement of God to man, specifically Adam. *"Be fruitful and multiply"* (Gen 1:28). After the flood, the first thing God said to Noah after he left the ark was: *"be fruitful and multiply"* (Gen 9:1). How about the last command of Jesus to his disciples in the gospel of Matthew? Same thing. Be fruitful and multiply—make disciples of all nations (Matt. 28:19-20). The concept and theme of multiplication is replete throughout the Bible, from Genesis to Revelation, from the first Adam to the last Adam, from King David to King Jesus, and from the patriarchs of Israel to the apostles of the church. Here's a sampling:

1. **Adam**	Gen. 1:28	"Be fruitful and multiply, and fill the earth. . ."[156]
2. **Noah**	Gen. 9:1, 7	"Be fruitful and multiply, and fill the earth."
3. **Abraham**	Gen. 17:2-6	"I will multiply you exceedingly. . . I will make you a father of a multitude of nations. . . I will make you exceedingly fruitful, and I will make nations of you."
	Gen. 22:17-18	"I will greatly multiply your seed as the stars of the heavens and the sand of the seashore. . .

In your seed all the nations of the earth shall be blessed. . ."

(*see also* Gen. 12:1-3; 13:16; 15:5-6; Ex. 32:13; Deut. 1:10-11; 10:22; Rom. 4:16-18; Gal. 6-9; Heb. 6:13-15; 11:12)

4. *Isaac*	Gen. 26:4	"I will multiply your descendants as the stars of heaven. . . and by your descendants all the nations of the earth shall be blessed."
	Gen. 28:3	"May God Almighty bless you and make you fruitful and multiply you, that you may be a company of peoples."
5. *Jacob*	Gen. 35:11	"Be fruitful and multiply; a nation and a company of nations shall come from you."
	Gen. 48:4	"Behold, I will make you fruitful and numerous, and I will make you a company of peoples. . ."
6. *Israel*	Ex. 1:7	"But the sons of Israel were fruitful and increased greatly, and multiplied. . ."

	Lev. 26:9	"So I will turn toward you and make you fruitful and multiply you. . ."
	Deut. 1:10	"The LORD your God has multiplied you, and behold, you are this day like the stars of heaven in number."
		(*see also* Deut. 6:3-7, 7:13, 8:1, 30:16; Isaiah 54:1-3, 59:21, 60:22; Jer. 23:3; 30:19; Ezek. 36:8-11)
7. David	Psalm 89:4	"I will establish your seed forever and build up your throne to all generations."
	Psalm 89:29	"So I will establish his descendants forever and his throne as the days of heaven."
	Jer. 33:22	"As the host of heaven cannot be counted and the sand of the sea cannot be measured, so I will multiply the descendants of David my servant. . ."
		(*see also* Psalm 89:35-36; 2 Sam. 7:12, 16; Ezek. 37:25-26)

8. *Jesus*	Isaiah 9:7	"There will be no end to the increase of His government. . ."
	Matt. 28:18-20	"Go therefore and make disciples of all the nations. . ."
		(*see also* Isaiah 9:2-3, 6, 61:1-4; Matt. 25:14-23; Luke 19:11-17; John 15:4-5, 8, 16; 17:18-21)
9. *The Church*	Acts 2:47	"And the Lord was adding to their number day by day those who were being saved."
	2 Tim. 2:2	"The things which you have heard from me. . ., entrust these to faithful men who will be able to teach others also."
		(*see also* Acts 9:31; 12:24; 1Cor. 3:6; 2 Cor. 9:10; 1 Thess. 1:6-8; Eph. 4:11-13; Rev. 7:9)

In the church age, spiritual multiplication is the process of generational growth among Christian disciples, both in terms of quantity and quality. It results from the spiritual investment by more-mature Christians in the lives of non-Christians and younger Christians, who come to faith, grow, mature and then spiritually reproduce. Spiritual multiplication therefore includes the ministries of evangelism, discipleship, and disciplemaking. Yet the term *spiritual multiplication* is a cumbersome and even boring description of a most vital and dynamic process. In fact, it's the highest form of *critical mass* on the planet!

The classic illustration of the power of spiritual multiplication is shown in the figure below, which compares the impact of spiritual addition to spiritual multiplication. Start with the left column, and imagine a gifted evangelist whose ability to win people to Christ is extraordinary. He travels the world preaching to multitudes, and seeing an average of ten people per day come to Christ. But he simply wins converts, leaving them for the next mass meeting in the next town. The right column depicts the discipleship ministry of one ordinary laborer. He invests in one other person, building them up to maturity over a year's time. At the end of that time there are two ordinary folks who reach out to two more people and invest in them over the next year.

Progress appears to be slow for the first few years compared to the work of the gifted evangelist. However, by year 17, the multiplying ministry of the ordinary laborer has exceeded that of the evangelist, and by year 25 the multiplying effect is so enormous as to completely dwarf the work of one evangelist. And that's the point. The gifted evangelist's ministry is performed solely by one person. The ordinary laborer, however, equips young disciples to do what he's doing, and the impact of multiple generations of disciples reaching and training new disciples has a staggering impact. Spiritual addition relies on the ministry of one gifted person. Spiritual multiplication relies on the ministry of ever-expanding generations of ordinary disciplemakers.

Spiritual Multiplication
v.
Spiritual Addition

No. of Converts (10 per day)	Year	No. of Disciples (1 per year)
3,650	1	1
7,300	2	2
10,950	3	4
14,600	4	8
18,300	5	16
21,900	6	32
25,550	7	64
29,200	8	128
32,850	9	256
36,500	10	512
40,100	11	1,024
43,800	12	2,048
47,400	13	4,096
51,100	14	8,193
54,750	15	16,384
58,400	16	32,768
60,225	17	65,536
63,875	18	131,072
67,525	19	262,144
71,175	20	524,288
74,825	21	1,048,576
78,475	22	2,097,152
82,125	23	4,194,304
85,775	24	8,388,608
89,425	25	16,777,216

Figure 2

At the 1989 Lausanne II Congress on World Evangelization in Manila, Ford Madison spoke on the subject of lay ministry. He started by surveying the audience as to who or what was most influential in leading them to faith in Christ. He first asked those to stand who had come to faith through some form of mass media, including radio, television, books, publications, etc., and a small percentage stood. He next asked those to stand who came to faith through some type of mass meeting or event, and again a small percentage stood. Finally, he asked those to stand who came to faith through the influence of an ordinary person, either a friend, parent, relative, or someone else. In response, 95% of the audience stood up. And among the first to stand with this group was a Greek Orthodox priest in full vestments and headdress! His point was to demonstrate the pervasive impact of spiritual multiplication through ordinary believers. He's used the same survey with other groups and churches, always with the same result.

On the 50th anniversary of his tenure as a professor at Dallas Theological Seminary in 2000, Dr. Howard Hendricks was interviewed by the seminary's alumni magazine. Dr. Hendricks, of course, is one of the most loved and respected teachers, speakers, and authors of our generation. He has ministered in one form or another all over the world. In the article, he was asked to describe his greatest contribution to God's work while at the seminary. He answered:

> I would say primarily my relationship with students. I've spent these 50 years primarily in discipleship and mentoring, and I think that's where my greatest contribution has been.[157]

He was also asked his favorite passage of Scripture, and he answered:

> Second Timothy 2:2, because I've always been committed to a ministry of multiplication. I

discovered that I can pastor one church, or I can train 20 guys to pastor 20 churches; I can go to one mission field or I can train 10 to go to 10 mission fields; I can teach in one school or train 5 guys to teach in 5 schools. So, based on that, "the things you've heard commit to faithful men" and women who are going to repeat the process.[158]

Dr. Hendricks is a true *spiritual patriarch*, discipling men for more than half a century. But he's done it the same way you and I can do it, by investing in a few people at a time over a lifetime, equipping them to be who he is and do what he does. While he's an extremely gifted speaker and teacher, he considers his greatest contribution to be the discipling of a few men at a time over the long haul. His ministry is a great example of the importance of spiritual multiplication. We certainly need gifted speakers, teachers, and evangelists, but we desperately need multiplying patriarchs. And they are few and far between.

Spiritual Decline

After studying the above illustration and thinking about the concept of spiritual multiplication, you may be wondering why the world hasn't been won for Christ three or four times over by now. Once you hit the 30, 40, and 50 year marks, the numbers should reach into the billions. This is not a new concept, and Christianity has been around for a while now. So why hasn't it happened? Why indeed? Tommy Nelson rightly points to the "*Killer D's*" as a contributing cause, and Dawson Trotman would agree.[159] Many disciples start their Christian lives and ministries well enough, only to get *distracted, discouraged,* or *disqualified.*

One man starts the race well, but somewhere along the way becomes distracted by the cares of this life or the deceitfulness of riches (Matt. 13:22). Or perhaps he's distracted by some good thing in and of itself, but it keeps him from pursuing the best things — things of eternal significance. He veers off the main path onto a side trail or a "rabbit trail," and therefore never reaches the goal of spiritual maturity and multiplication. He is distracted from his walk in Christ and therefore never matures to the point that he bears lasting fruit (John 15:2, 16).

Another man also starts his race well, but a series of events overwhelms him with discouragement, and he falls out of the race (Matt. 13:21). His roots may not have been deep enough, or his expectations were too idealistic, or he encounters severe hardship and suffering. Discouragement drains away his life as he loses focus on Christ. Perhaps he's overcome by anxiety, failing to rely on God and the peace that surpasses human understanding (Phil. 4:6-7). He fails to meditate on the things that are true and right and good (Phil. 4:8), and his spiritual progress terminates.

And still another man starts well, but becomes disqualified when he falls headlong into sin. Somewhere along the path he becomes ensnared by the lust of the flesh, the lust of the eyes, or the boastful pride of life (1 John 2:15-16). He loses credibility and his qualifications to serve or lead, and is forced out of the race. He fails to continue walking in the Spirit by making provision for the flesh in regard to its lusts (Gal. 5:16; Rom. 13:14). And if he fails to repent, his life remains spiritually sterile.

In each of these three instances, the person fails to reach a critical mass of spiritual growth that leads to spiritual multiplication. There are other causes of spiritual sterility, of course, but the results are the same. The growth and reproductive process withers like a dead branch on a vine (John 15:2, 6). Every branch that continues to abide in the vine, however, bears much fruit and shows itself to be a reproducing disciple (John 15:8, 16). But it's also important to remember that the vine does not grow in the controlled environment of a pristine greenhouse. Rather, it grows in the toxic, polluted soil of a nuclear war zone. Because, in case you hadn't heard, there's a war on! Sin has entirely corrupted the planet, and the enemy's out to destroy the entirety of creation, especially the church. He fails, of course, but there will be casualties, and that underscores the broader hindrance to spiritual multiplication—apostasy.

I've discussed critical mass in the contexts of personal growth and spiritual multiplication as processes that build and edify the church. Apostasy has the exact opposite effect—it tears down, nullifies, and destroys the church. Scripture repeatedly warns of the danger of apostasy (Matt. 24:4-12; Acts 20:29-30; 2 Thess. 2:3-12; 1 Tim. 4:1-3; 2 Tim. 3:1-9). It also teaches that during the period between the first and second comings of Christ, the overall situation will degenerate, reaching a climax shortly before Christ's return.[160] "The Spirit clearly says that in later times some will abandon the faith and follow deceiving spirits and things taught by demons" (1 Tim. 4:1, NIV). For in the last days, men will be "lovers of themselves, lovers of money, boastful, proud,. . . unholy, without love,. . . without self-control,. . . conceited, lovers of pleasure rather than lovers of God—having a form of godliness but denying its power" (2 Tim. 3:1-5, NIV).

In fact, the day of the Lord itself will not come until the final apostasy comes first (2 Thess. 2:3). Dr. Lewis Sperry Chafer once observed:

> All that God commits to men seems to follow the downward course of declension. This was true of Israel, it is declared even of Gentile authority which began as gold and ends as iron and clay, it is true likewise of the professing church. . . . The elect company of true believers is ever beset with tendencies to formality, unbelief, and worldliness. This condition, as predicted, has continued throughout the age.[161]

As far back as King Nebuchadnezzar's dream of the great statue in Daniel 2, prophecy and history have shown that human history tends toward decline, not glory. As Dr. Duguid noted in his commentary of the book of Daniel:

> The progression of world history is typically not upward to glory and unity but rather downward to dishonor and disunity. Thus the statue progresses from gold, to silver, to bronze, to iron, and from one head, to a chest and arms, to a belly and thighs, to feet and toes of composite iron and clay. . . . In contrast, God's kingdom grows from humble beginnings to ultimate, united glory as a single kingdom that fills the whole earth forever.[162]

Abraham & Charlie

In spite of the countervailing forces against spiritual multiplication, God's plan is not hindered in the least. He will accomplish everything he set out to do. His kingdom will prevail, and both Habakkuk 2:14 and Isaiah 11:9 will come true: "the earth *shall* be filled with the knowledge of the glory of the LORD, as the waters cover the sea." As Dawson Trotman stressed years ago, we have no better illustration of the ultimate pervasiveness of God's glory than the fact that water covers every inch of the sea! Let me close then by telling the story of two men, Abraham, the original patriarch, and Charlie Riggs, a modern patriarch and true citizen soldier from the "greatest generation."

The man who became, and whose name meant, "the father of many nations" went by another name most of his life. I've talked about him in previous chapters, but I need to offer a few more observations. Abram was a simple, albeit highly successful livestock rancher. Wherever he went, he seemed to prosper, but he was not an ambitious or arrogant empire builder. He deferred to lesser men on occasion, in particular his nephew Lot on the choice of livestock range. He feared being killed by two kings because his wife was unusually attractive. But we really don't know that much about him beyond the general narrative of Genesis 11 – 25. So what made this man so special that everything seems to trace back to him? The three major monotheistic religions refer to him as "Father Abraham." This man was so unique that God made to him the most extraordinary promises ever made to an ordinary man. But why him?

On the surface, he just doesn't seem that impressive. He did some good things, and he seems to have trusted God a few times, but nothing all that earth-shattering. Okay, the Isaac-sacrifice incident, though peculiar to us in modern times, shows an unusual sense of trust and obedience. But can we really imagine God requiring someone to sacrifice a son? That's a pagan practice that God was totally against, except of course when it involved his own son! Yet, as we consider Abraham, I come back to my observation that sometimes the simplest truths are the most profound. What sets him apart is so simple that it almost gets overlooked.

Abraham *believed* God. No, let me phrase it like a lawyer would: in the absence of corroborating physical evidence of any kind, Abraham believed and *kept on* believing God. Or, I could say it this way: in the face of overwhelming evidence to the contrary, Abraham believed God. *Simple faith.* Abraham had a simple faith that moved him to leave his homeland and family and go to a distant land. He left not even knowing where he was going. But he believed and therefore obeyed God. He was told he would have descendants too numerous to count, but it was *25 more years* before he had his *first* promised son (Gen. 12:4; 21:5). And when that promise was made, his wife was well past child-bearing years. To anyone else, it would have been ridiculous to think that God would give this old couple a child of their own. But he said he would, and Abraham believed it. "Now faith is the assurance of things hoped for, the conviction of things not seen" (Heb. 11:1, NASB).

After overcoming all these odds against having even one son, Abraham was then presented with the ultimate test—to sacrifice his son simply because God said so. Even if I could get past the harshness of such a command, I think it would utterly confuse and crush my confidence in God to wait a lifetime for one promised son, and then sacrifice him. But that's not how Abraham responded. He believed that God would simply raise his promised son from the dead after the sacrifice (Heb. 11:17-19). I can think of no more radical faith. And that's the single defining characteristic of a true patriarch—he *believes* God against all odds and all circumstances, and acts accordingly. His faith is based on God's express promises. It's not blind faith based on presumption or speculation. It's grounded on the word of God.

God of course does the actual work of spiritual multiplication, but he uses men to fulfill his promise to build a kingdom of his son's followers across all generations. Abraham was the first man to receive that promise (Rom. 4:16; Gal. 3:16). "And so from this one man, and he as good as dead, came descendants as numerous as the stars in the sky and as countless as the sand on the seashore" (Heb. 11:12, NIV). Abraham had only one promised son, but his grandson Jacob went down into Egypt with 70 descendants (Exodus 1:5). After Joseph, his brothers, and that generation died, "the Israelites were fruitful and multiplied greatly and became exceedingly numerous, so that the land was filled with them" (Exodus 1:7, NIV).

Forty years after the exodus, on the border of the Promised Land, Moses apprised Israel, "Your forefathers who went down into Egypt were seventy in all, and now the LORD your God has made you as numerous as the stars in the sky" (Deut. 10:22, NIV). Abraham didn't live to see it all happen, but it happened! "Against all hope, Abraham in hope believed and so became the father of many nations" (Rom. 4:18, NIV). And all those who are of faith are sons of Abraham (Gal. 3:7), because Christ is the promised blessing of Abraham to all the nations (Gal. 3:14, 16). For himself,

Abraham was fully convinced that God had the power to do what he promised (Rom. 4:21), and so became part of the greatest enterprise in human history!

That enterprise carries on today, and as E. M. Bounds famously said, while men are always looking for better methods, God is looking for better men, because *men* are God's method![163] Charlie Riggs was one of those men, and among the more significant patriarchs in recent history. To tell his story though, I need to add some context. Around 1950 when Billy Graham was beginning his evangelistic crusades, he approached Dawson Trotman to ask him to help with the follow-up portion of the crusades. Graham had studied the great evangelists and revivals, and found that none of them had any real follow-up to their ministries. He saw the value of Trotman's follow-up discipleship ministry and wanted it to be part of his crusades. Trotman, however, initially refused, stating that he worked with individuals and small groups, and was just too busy to help with crusades.[164]

Trotman told Graham that he'd simply have to get someone else. But Graham would not be refused, gripping Trotman by both shoulders and asking: "Who else? Who else is majoring in this? You are the only one I know who is majoring in follow-up." So after much prayer, Trotman agreed to help and assigned Lorne Sanny to be the point person for The Navigators in their partnership with the Billy Graham Evangelistic Association (BGEA). The Navigators thereafter developed and implemented BGEA's follow-up strategy.[165] (Sanny succeeded Trotman as president of The Navigators after Trotman's accidental death in 1956.)

Daws began discipling Lorne in 1941, and sent him to Seattle in 1944 on his first solo assignment to work with servicemen. The ministry was tough and Lorne had only one soldier who regularly attended his Friday night Bible study, "a square-jawed lieutenant who listened carefully and said little." When Daws later checked on Lorne's progress, Lorne was deeply disappointed to report that he had only one man to disciple. But Daws surprised him by telling him to invest his life in *that one man!*[166] That one man was Charlie Riggs, one of the most fruitful disciplemakers of his generation.

As a young man, Charlie worked in the oil fields and other jobs until he was 25. In World War II, he rose from the rank of private to first lieutenant, but did the work of a colonel at his last post in Seattle, Washington. There, he met Lorne who discipled him, an experience that super-charged Riggs' spiritual life. His personal devotion to Christ meshed with the discipline and total commitment that marked his Army life. He grew tremendously during these years under Lorne's leadership. After Lorne assumed responsibility for the follow-up at the BGEA crusades in 1950, he asked Charlie to join his team.[167]

The Navigators directed the BGEA's follow-up efforts until 1957 when the latter created its own counseling and follow-up department, with Charlie as its director. He served in that role for more than 30 years. He and those he mentored trained pastors and laymen in dozens of countries. Around the world, thousands grew from and applied what they learned in Charlie's training through their churches. In fact, he was responsible for the training of more people in basic follow-up ministry than any other person of his generation. He developed a simple tool and booklet for sharing the gospel used by the BGEA for many years, *Steps to Peace With God.* He also developed the BGEA's small group Bible study, *Thirty Discipleship Exercises, The Pathway to Christian Maturity.*[168]

Among the men he personally discipled, Charlie modeled a husband who treasured his wife and a dad who played with his kids. He was a consistent pacesetter, always seeking to apply Scripture to his own life, and sharing something fresh from his time alone with God. His life of uncompromising obedience was a constant challenge to his men. He faithfully challenged and encouraged them, directly and honestly sharing needs he saw in their lives. He led them in weekly inductive Bible study, seeking personal applications. He used to say: "You don't have a ministry. Your *life* is your ministry."[169] In other words, your life speaks far more powerfully than your words. Franklin Graham wrote of him:

> Charlie was an author, teacher, prayer warrior, mentor and friend to many. He modeled the life of a Christian soldier and left his mark on all those with whom he invested his time and wisdom. He was honest, direct and stretched people to be all they could be in Christ and encouraged them to use Scripture in application to everyday life.[170]

This quiet, rough-neck oilfield worker was used mightily by God, according to his own prayer, "for Christ to get all the glory and honor." Among the many men he discipled were Oklahoma businessman, Gene Warr, and Baptist minister, Dr. Waylon Moore, both highly influential patriarchs in their own right. Even after his retirement, he volunteered in a prison ministry, leading a Bible study for inmates. A true patriarch and life-time laborer, Charlie Riggs finished his race in 2008 at age 91.[171] As a humble man of tremendous spiritual power, he embodied the principle of critical mass, classically illustrated in Isaiah 60:22. "A little one shall become a thousand, and a small one a strong nation. I, the LORD, will hasten it in its time" (Isaiah 60:22, NKJV).

About the Author

S hane Sanders is an attorney, practicing in central Texas. He's married to Janet, and they have three grown children, starting families of their own. He served for many years on staff with The Navigators, leading collegiate and church discipleship ministries in College Station and Waco, and on the board of Frontier Camp near Crockett.

He's also served variously as an elder, deacon, small groups' leader, and men's discipleship leader at his churches in Waco and College Station. He's also a guest lecturer in the seminary disciplemaking course at Southwestern in Fort Worth.

Shane's ministry passions include one-to-one and small group discipleship, men's leadership development, and speaking opportunities to promote them. He also loves to incorporate American history into ministry training.

Endnotes

Chapter 1

[1] John Frederick Dorman, *Adventurers of Purse and Person Virginia 1607-1624/5*, Fourth Edition, Volume One (2004), 702-711; Virginia McKinney Turner, *The Cobb Family of "Rocky Mount" Piney Flats, Tennessee 1613-1972* (1973), 1-4.

[2] James Horn, *A Land As God Made It: Jamestown and the Birth of America* (2005), 212-216, 225-232; Benjamin Woolly, *Savage Kingdom* (2007), 310-313, 329-339.

[3] Horn, 178-181; David A. Price, *Love & Hate in Jamestown* (2003), 128-129, 137-140.

[4] Ibid.

[5] www.wikipedia.org (*critical mass*) (accessed 2009).

[6] Jim Collins, *Good to Great* (2001), 12.

[7] Ibid., 182.

[8] Ibid., 186.

[9] Ibid., 164-165.

[10] Ibid., 165.

[11] Bruce L. Shelley, *Church History in Plain Language* (1982), 256-257.

[12] E. M. Bounds, *Power Through Prayer* (1912), 1.

[13] Stephen E. Ambrose, *D-Day* (1994), 24-25.

[14] Ibid.

[15] Leroy Eims, *The Lost Art of Disciple Making* (1978), 45.

[16] Ibid., 45-46.

Chapter 2

[17] Martin Campbell, Director, *The Mask of Zorro* (1998).

[18] Spiros Zodhiates, *The Complete Word Study Dictionary New Testament* (1992), 936.

[19] Alan Hirsch, *The Forgotten Ways* (2006), 121-123; *The Forgotten Ways Handbook* (2009), 20-21.

[20] Ibid.

[21] Hirsch, *The Forgotten Ways Handbook*, 21; *The Forgotten Ways*, 122-123.

[22] Ibid.

[23] A.J. Langguth, *Patriots, The Men Who Started the American Revolution* (1988), 42-43; Wythe House Curator, Williamsburg, Va. (2007).

[24] Willard Sterne Randall, *Thomas Jefferson, A Life* (1993), 45-55.

[25] Ibid.

[26] Ibid., 52.

[27] Ibid., 53-55.

[28] Ibid., 47, 55.

[29] Ibid., 265-278, 287-288, 361, 376, 566-570.

[30] Arthur M. Schlesinger, Jr., *A Thousand Days, John F. Kennedy in the White House* (1965), 733.

[31] Randall, 48; Hugh Howard, *Houses of the Founding Fathers* (2007), 20.

[32] Shelley, 326.

[33] Ibid., 326-348.

[34] Robert D. Foster, *The Navigator* (1983), 2, back cover.

[35] Foster, 115; Betty Lee Skinner, *Daws* (1974), 76.

[36] Foster, 114-115; Skinner, 76.

[37] Skinner, 82-83; Foster, 78, 115-116.

[38] *The Navigators Insiders Guide* (2002).

[39] Foster, 124; Skinner, 70.

[40] Foster, 127-128.

[41] Ibid.; *Insider's Guide*; Skinner, 61.

[42] Skinner, 384-385.

[43] See Chapter 9.

Chapter 3

[44] William D. Mounce and Robert H. Mounce, editors, *Greek and English Interlinear New Testament (NASB/NIV), [Greek-English Dictionary]* (2008), 1177.

[45] Ibid; Zodhiates, 1372-1373; Richard C. Trench, *Synonyms of the New Testament* (1989), 89-91; W. E. Vine, *Vine's Concise Dictionary of Bible Words* (1985), 274.

[46] Mounce, 1091; Zodhiates, 834.

[47] Mounce, 1165; Zodhiates, 1308.

[48] Mounce, 1180; Zodhiates, 1394.

[49] Dave Kraft, *Leaders Who Last* (2004), 72.

[50] Charles F. Pfeiffer and Everett F Harrison, editors, *The Wycliffe Bible Commentary* (1962), 1311.

Chapter 4

[51] Oswald Chambers, *My Utmost for His Highest* (1935), 184.

[52] A. W. Tozer, *The Pursuit of God* (1982), 15.

[53] *See* The Navigator's Hand Illustration, <u>www.navigators.org</u>.

[54] Betty Lee Skinner, *With Integrity of Heart and Skillful Hand* (1998), 107-108.

Chapter 5

[55] William Barclay, *The Gospel of Matthew,* Volume 1 (1975), 397.

[56] Zodhiates, 960.

[57] Mounce, 1112.

[58] John F. Walvoord, Roy B. Zuck, eds., *The Bible Knowledge Commentary, New Testament* (2000), 324; John MacArthur, *The MacArthur Bible Commentary* (2005), 1406.

[59] MacArthur, 1676; Walvoord, 608; Vines, 272.

[60] Ibid.

[61] Ibid.

[62] Walvoord, 632, 682; Merrill F. Unger, *The New Unger's Bible Dictionary* (1985) 251, 596, 623; Zodhiates, 1306, 1328.

[63] Ibid.

[64] R. C. Sproul, *The Holiness of God* (1985), 57.

[65] Sproul, 54-55.

[66] Richard C. Trench, *Synonyms of the New Testament* (1876), 346.

[67] *See* Tommy Nelson, *The Footprints of God; History of the Church, Part 12* (1999), www.dbcmedia.com; Dagobert Runes, ed., *Treasure of Philosophy* (1955), 1028-1029.

[68] William Barclay, *The Letter to the Romans* (1975), 155-158.

[69] D. Guthrie et al., eds., *The New Bible Commentary, Revised* (1970), 1040.

[70] Walvoord, 486; Barclay, 158.

[71] MacArthur, 1695-1696.

[72] Guthrie, 1118.

[73] Jerry Bridges, *The Pursuit of Holiness* (1978), 13-14, 22.

Chapter 6

[74] Trench, 57-59; Zodhiates, 64-67; MacArthur, 1676.

[75] Ibid.

[76] Clint Black, *Something That We Do* (1997).

[77] Gary Desalvo, Men's Retreat (2010).

Chapter 7

[78] Dr. Norman Geisler, *Systematic Theology, Volume One* (2002), 229, 235.

[79] Dr. Charles C. Ryrie, *A Survey of Bible Doctrine* (1972), 7.

[80] Dr. Ray Van Neste, 2 Tim. 3:16 *Study Notes,* The ESV Study Bible (2008), 2342.

[81] Walvoord, 757.

[82] Geisler, *Volume One*, 241.

[83] Ibid., 235-237.

[84] www.wordiQ.com (*hermeneutics, exegesis*)(accessed 2012).

[85] www.Theopedia.com (*exegesis*)(accessed 2012).

86 Ibid.

87 Ibid., (*hermeneutics*).

88 www.wordiQ.com (*hermeneutics*)(accessed 2012); Dr. Grant Kaul, *Living the Word* (unpublished paper), 12.

89 Kaul, 11-12, 24.

90 Dr. William Barclay, *The Letter to the Romans, Revised Edition* (1975), 69.

91 MacArthur, 1516.

92 *Merriam-Webster Dictionary* (2012); Geisler, *Volume One,* 15.

93 Dr. Norman Geisler, *Systematic Theology, Volume Two* (2003), 17-406, and Scripture cites therein; Dr. R. C. Sproul, *Now, That's a Good Question!* (1996), 6-27; Ryrie, 11-35, and Scripture cites therein.

94 Geisler, *Volume Two,* 278-279, 290-291, and Scripture cites therein; Ryrie, 29-34, and Scripture cites therein.

95 C.S. Lewis, *Mere Christianity* (1952), 55.

96 Vine, 59; Zodhiates, 1107; John 14:16, *The NET Bible, Second Beta Edition* (2003), 1943, tn17.

97 *See* Ryrie, 67-88; Sproul, 53-72.

98 Geisler, *Volume Two,* 441.

99 *See* Ibid., 423-458; Ryrie, 100-104.

100 www.wikipedia (accessed 2012).

101 *See* Tommy Nelson, *The Footprints of God; History of the Church* (1999), and *Step by Step: The Road to Darkness* (2004), www.dbcmedia.com.

102 *See* Ibid.

Chapter 8

103 Zodhiates, 430.

104 Collins, 96.

105 Ibid., 97, 90-91.

106 Ibid., 90-91.

107 Skinner, *Daws,* 384-385.

108 Walvoord, 533.

109 *See* J. Oswald Sanders, *The Holy Spirit and His Gifts* (1970); Lloyd Edwards, *Discerning Your Spiritual Gifts* (1988); Ray

C. Stedman, *Body Life* (1995); Henry and Mel Blackaby, *What's So Spiritual About Your Gifts* (2004); MacArthur, 1590-1597; Walvoord, 532-535; Geisler, *Volume Four*, 187-214.

[110] Leon Morris, *Luke, An Introduction and Commentary* (1988), 302.

[111] Dr. William Barclay, *The Gospel of Luke* (1975), 238.

[112] Dr. William Barclay, *The Gospel of Matthew, Volume 2* (1975), 324.

[113] Walvoord, 94.

Chapter 9

[114] Philip Schaff, *History of the Christian Church, Volume 7* (1888), p. 16-26.

[115] Dr. John R. Stott, www.worklife.org.

[116] John Pollack, *The Apostle, A Life of Paul* (1972), 15, 18; Rev. James Stalker, *Life of St. Paul* (1912), 22-23.

[117] Bruce Catton and William B. Catton, *The Bold and Magnificent Dream, America's Founding Years, 1492-1815* (1978), 387.

[118] James Thomas Flexner, *Washington, The Indispensable Man* (1969), 79, 111.

[119] David McCullough, *1776* (2005), 20, 53, 58,

[120] Flexner, 157.

[121] Ibid, 178-179 (emphasis added).

[122] McCullough, 293-294.

[123] Ron Chernow, *Washington, A Life* (2010), 457-458 (emphasis added).

[124] Stephen E. Ambrose, *D-Day, June 6, 1944: The Climactic Battle of World War II* (1994), 25, 40.

[125] Stephen E. Ambrose, *Band of Brothers* (1992), 15 (emphasis added).

[126] Ibid., 21

[127] Ibid., 15-16.

[128] Larry Alexander, *Biggest Brother, The Life of Major Dick Winters, The Man Who Led the Band of Brothers* (2005), 20-38.
[129] Ambrose, *Band of Brothers*, 88.
[130] Alexander, 118-124; Ambrose, *Band of Brothers*, 147-153.
[131] Alexander, 123-124; Ambrose, *Band of Brothers*, 152, 290, [300] (emphasis added).
[132] Elisabeth Elliot, Ed., *The Journals of Jim Elliot* (1978), 174.

Chapter 10

[133] Dr. Robert E. Coleman, *The Master Plan of Evangelism* (1963), 41.
[134] Ibid., 45.
[135] Ibid., 45-46.

Chapter 11

[136] Skinner, *With Integrity of Heart and Skillful Hand*, 131.
[137] C. John Collins, *ESV Study Notes* (2008), Psalm 78:65-72, 1037.
[138] www.wikipedia.com, *Pathfinder (military)* (accessed 2012).
[139] MacArthur, 1714.
[140] John Bunyan (retold by James H. Thomas), *Pilgrim's Progress* (1964), 12-13, 22-27, 87-89.
[141] Kraft, 105-108.
[142] Ibid., 106.
[143] Ibid., 108.
[144] Ibid. (emphasis added), 107.
[145] Ibid., 105.
[146] Zodhiates, 843; Mounce, 1093.
[147] Ambrose, *D-Day*, 168, 278-279 (emphasis added).
[148] David Maraniss, *When Pride Still Mattered, A Life of Vince Lombardi* (1999), 250, 437, 458, 503.
[149] Ibid., 34-37, 300.
[150] Ibid., 35-36; Ray Robinson, *Rockne of Notre Dame, The Making of a Football Legend* (1999), 152.

[151] Maraniss, 36, 63, 225; Robinson, 65,112.

[152] Robinson, 138, 262.

[153] Maraniss, 99, 101.

[154] Robinson, 162; Maraniss, 333.

[155] Maraniss, 103.

Chapter 12

[156] All verses in 1 through 9 are NASB.

[157] Dallas Theological Seminary, *Connection, A Ministry to Alumni of DTS* (Spring 2000), Vol. 7, No. 4.

[158] Ibid.

[159] Tommy Nelson, *The Lost Art of Disciplemaking* (2002), www.dbcmedia.com; Dawson Trotman, *Born to Reproduce* (1955), www.discipleshiplibrary.com.

[160] MacArthur, 1789; Walvoord, 739.

[161] Dr. Lewis Sperry Chafer, *Systematic Theology, Volume IV* (1948), 353.

[162] Dr. Iain M. Duguid, *ESV Study Notes* (2008), Daniel 2:43-44, 1590.

[163] Bounds, 1.

[164] Foster, 129-131; Trotman, *Born to Reproduce*.

[165] Ibid.

[166] Ibid.; Skinner, *With Integrity of Heart and Skillful Hands*, 22-29.

[167] Dr. Waylon B. Moore, *Great Mentors I Have Known: Charlie Riggs, Pacesetter* (2008), www.mentoring-disciples.org; Rebecca K. Grosenbach, *Charlie Riggs: Lifelong Laborer* (2008), www.navigators.org.

[168] Ibid.

[169] Ibid.; Rex Keener, *The Legacy of Charlie Riggs* (2008), www.rexkeener.com; Gene Warr, *Making Disciples* (1990), 20.

[170] Keener.

[171] Moore; Grosenbach; Keener; Warr, 20.

CPSIA information can be obtained
at www.ICGtesting.com
Printed in the USA
BVHW03s1934140918
527557BV00001B/7/P